MARK

A SELF-STUDY GUIDE

Irving L. Jensen

MOODY PRESS
CHICAGO

ISBN: 0-8024-4465-2

Printed in the United States of America

Contents

Introduction

Two practical questions frequently asked by students of a book of the Bible are: "Where do I begin?" and, "How do I proceed?" An illustration of how important these questions are is found in sports, where a good finish of a race depends on a good start and a strong pace along the way. Bible study can be likened to this. A good start and a steady advance are the makings of profitable Bible study. The purpose of this manual is to help the Bible student in both of these areas. For example, the first two starter lessons are devoted to background and survey, to help you get the feel of Mark's gospel; the remaining lessons are your guides in searching the Scripture text of the sixteen chapters. Each of these latter lessons is broken down into six parts:

1. *Preparation for study.* Suggestions given here will help you get that *initial* momentum for studying the passage.

2. *Analysis.* This is the core of your independent study. The manual's contribution is mainly through "search" questions and directions.

3. *Notes.* These notes are usually facts or interpretations not available from the Bible passage itself.

4. *For thought and discussion.* Application of the Bible text is the main appeal here. If you are studying in a group, open discussion of the subjects will be profitable.

5. *Further study.* Subjects for extended studies beyond the manual's lesson are suggested here.

6. *Words to ponder.* A phrase of the Bible text set off by itself can often be revealing. This pause at the end of each lesson is our reminder of the importance of *meditation* on God's holy Word.

Independent Bible Study

Independent Bible study goes hand in hand with instruction received from others. This is clearly illustrated by the example of the Berean Christians under Paul's ministry. Luke writes that these young Christians were "more open-minded than the people in Thessalonica," for "they listened to the message with great eagerness, and every day they studied the Scriptures to see if what Paul said was really true" (Acts 17:11; *Today's English Version*). This involvement in personal, firsthand study of the Bible is practical for everyone (for the Bible is everyman's book), and it is profitable to all (for the joy of firsthand discovery escapes no one).

The procedures of independent Bible study are simple yet basic:

OBSERVATION (What does the text say?)
INTERPRETATION (What does it mean?)
APPLICATION (How am I involved?)

All the study questions given in this manual are geared to those areas of your study. Keep in mind John Wycliffe's famous maxim concerning the foundational stage of OBSERVATION: "It shall greatly helpe ye to understande Scripture if thou mark not only what is spoken or wrytten, but of whom and to whom, with what words, at what time, where, to what intent, with what circumstances, considering what goeth before and what followeth."

Tools for Study

A good craftsman works with good tools. Here is a recommended minimal list of tools for effective Bible study:

1. *A study edition of the Bible.* Large print, high-quality paper and marginal space for notations are earmarks of a good study Bible. Cross references are also desirable. The version consistently referred to by this manual is the King James.

2. *A good modern version of the Bible.* A modern version is helpful for seeing (1) the movement of thought in a particular passage and (2) various shades of meaning intended by the original Greek word of the New Testament text. Do all your analysis in your basic study edition; refer to the modern version for comparative studies.

3. *Paper and pencil for recording observations.* "The pencil is one of the best eyes." It will surprise you how many new vistas appear in your study once you begin to record your observations on paper. *This cannot be overemphasized.*

4. *Outside helps.* A good commentary is especially helpful for background and for light on problem passages.[1] Complete most of your independent study of any one particular passage before consulting the commentary. An exhaustive concordance is invaluable.

1. *Length of study units.* You as leader of the class should determine how much of each lesson should be studied at each meeting of the group.

2. *Homework.* Urge each member of the group to complete the analysis suggestions of the manual before meeting together. This includes writing out answers whenever possible. It is important that each member think and study for himself so that he can weigh more accurately what someone else says about a Bible text. Encourage the asking of questions. Never underestimate the significance of a question asked, regardless of its type. It is a healthy sign of mental activity when questions are asked, and Bible teaching is more pertinent in an environment of searching.

3. *Bible references.* Emphasize the importance of reading all the Scripture references, including those outside the book of Mark.

4. *Survey chart.* The survey Chart D should be thoroughly studied by all members of the group. Refer to it frequently for context and review. A chalkboard, poster paper, or overhead projector can be used to advantage here.

5. *Analytical charts.*[2] Analytical charts, whether done briefly or in detail, can be developed in the group session with everyone suggesting words, phrases, and outlines to be recorded on the chart. The possibilities are endless as to what may be done with this video form.

6. *The class hour.* Devote most of the time to group discussion of the Bible text. Avoid the straight lecture approach. Encourage participation in discussion by *all* members. At the beginning of the meeting, review the main parts of the previous lesson. At the close of the discussion, emphasize especially the practical application of the truths learned.

7. *The opening meeting.* Spend time in the first group session discussing ways to study the Bible profitably. Consider the importance of prayer and a dependency on the teaching ministry of the Holy Spirit. Also discuss what each of these has to do with effective Bible study:

1. *The Wycliffe Bible Commentary*, edited by Charles F. Pfeiffer and Everett F. Harrison, is highly recommended as a companion aid in this self-study series.
2. The analytical chart method is described in detail in the author's book *Independent Bible Study* (Chicago: Moody, 1963).

THIRST   TIME
TOIL   TEACHABLENESS

"And a voice came out of the cloud, saying, This is my beloved Son: hear him. And suddenly, when they had looked round
about, they saw no man any more, save *Jesus only*" (Mark 9:7-8).
May your study of the book of Mark give you a vision of Jesus such
as you have never experienced before.

Lesson 1

Background

For a few decades after Christ's ascension, the world did not have the full written gospel record. During those years the redemptive message of the gospel was being proclaimed by word of mouth (read Acts 15:7), based on truthworthy recollections of eyewitnesses. And at least some of those recollections were being written out on scrolls for a more permanent record. We do not know the exact circumstances of the writing of each of the four gospels, but we are confident that each appeared on schedule according to a divine plan.

In the case of the gospel of Mark, it is generally held that Peter was Mark's informant of eyewitness stories about Jesus. It is possible that Peter was referring to this forthcoming manuscript by Mark when he wrote 2 Peter 1:15. (Read the verse in the context of its two preceding verses.) In this first lesson we will be studying this and other aspects of the background of the actual writing of Mark, so that we will feel more at home when we begin to study the Bible text itself. In Lesson 2 we will move to the next stage of Bible study, which is a survey of the whole book. Then we will be ready for our main task, which is analyzing in detail the Bible text of all sixteen chapters (Lessons 3-14). This study guide thus follows the standard order of procedure for Bible study, which is:

1. becoming acquainted with the BACKGROUND of the book's writing (Lesson 1)

2. making a general SURVEY of the book's contents (Lesson 2)

3. examining each part, in detailed ANALYSIS (Lessons 3-14)

I. BACKGROUND

A. The Man Mark

Although the human author is not identified in the gospel, internal evidence from the text itself agrees with the external witness of the early church Fathers that John Mark was the author.[1] This is the man cited by name in the following New Testament passages: Acts 12:12, 25; 13:5, 13; 15:37-39; 1 Peter 5:13; Colossians 4:10; Philemon 23-24; 2 Timothy 4:11.

1. *Birth and early life.* Mark was born some ten to fifteen years after Jesus of Nazareth and Saul of Tarsus, so he may have been a late teenager at the time of the crucial events of Jesus' public ministry. His parents gave him the Hebrew name John (Hebrew, *Johanan,* "Jehovah is gracious"), and his Roman surname Mark[2] (cf. Acts 15:37) may have been adopted at a later time in his life.

In Colossians 4:10 (NASB*) we read that Mark was a cousin of Barnabas, a key person in Acts 4–15. Mark's mother, Mary, was a devout woman of prosperous means. Her home, which may have been located in the valley of Kidron near the Garden of Gethsemane, was dedicated to God. This is confirmed by Luke, who records in Acts 12:12-17 that in the early days of the Christian church, after James the Elder had been slain by Herod Agrippa, and while Peter was in prison for the testimony of the gospel, she was courageous and faithful to the extent of letting her house be the meeting place for the local believers. And who knows but that Jesus visited this home during His lifetime and even partook of the Last Supper there?

Many believe that the unnamed "young man" of Mark 14:51 was Mark himself. (Read Mark 14:43-52.) E.M. Blaiklock suggests this imagined (though not impossible) story behind the Mark account:

> In the long room on the roof of the house of Mary, the rich widow lady of Jerusalem, the Lord and His band meet for what was to be the Last Supper. In his room below, awake and alert, for he sensed the danger which lurked about the house, lay Mary's son, John Mark. He heard the hurried steps of Judas on the stair

*New American Standard Bible.

1. Among these are the Greek Fathers Papias (A.D. 70-155), Justin Martyr (A.D. 100-165), Clement of Alexandria (A.D. 150-217), Irenaeus (A.D. 120-102), Origen (A.D. 185-254), Eusebius (A.D. 270-340); and the Latin Fathers Tertullian (A.D. 150-220) and Jerome (A.D. 340-420). (Most dates are approximate.)
2. The Greek *Markos* is from the Latin *markus,* "large hammer."

way without, and listened with sharper care. And then the noise of feet, and the rest depart.

On a sudden impulse the boy seizes a linen sheet from his bed, wraps it round his body and follows. He watches under the olive trees, sure that some crisis is at hand. A flare of torches, and the betrayer is there. With a boy's reckless loyalty he shouts some protest, and angry hands lay hold of him. Slipping out of his sheet Mark escapes. Perhaps he bore a cruel and mutilating sword-slash across his fingers, for an old tradition says that in the early Church Mark was called "the Stumpfingered."[3]

Indelible were the impressions being made as young John Mark grew up in the environs of a professing "holy" city and in the shelter of a genuinely devout home. He must have been an eyewitness of some events of Jesus' life. He could not escape crossing the trail of the Son of God. And all the while he was being prepared for a later work in the service of the gospel, studying the Scriptures and learning the languages current in the stream of the metropolis—Aramaic, Greek, and Latin.

Mary had a house and a family, and they were given to God. And God had a Son and a gospel, and they were given to the world. Mary's Mark and God's gospel were brought together, and millions of souls since then have cherished the possession of this, the gospel according to Mark.

2. *Conversion.* Though the devout Judaistic heritage formulated the recollections of Mark's earlier life, there came the day in his life when, like his mother, he was confronted with the claims of the man of Galilee and was compelled to answer the question, "Who do *you* say that I am?" (cf. 8:29). Peter may have been the disciple used of God to lead Mark to Christ, and this may be why Peter speaks of Mark as "Mark my son" (1 Pet. 5:13). Details of Mark's conversion experience, however, are not given in the New Testament record.

3. *Christian ministry.* Two gospel writers, Matthew and John, were apostles of Jesus. The other two, Mark and Luke, were not of the chosen twelve. The New Testament verses where Mark's name appears reveal some of the highlights of Mark's experience in Christian service.

Read each passage, and the context surrounding it, and record biographical notes about Mark in each case.

Observe among other things the variety of co-laborers, and the fact of Paul's and Mark's reconciliation after the separation of Acts 13:13. What do you think helped Mark to mature spiritually be-

3. E.M. Blaiklock, *Mark: The Man and His Message*, p. 9-10.

Passage	Date A.D.	Place[4] and Ministry	Colaborers
Acts 12:12, 25	46		
13:5	47		
13:13	47		
15:37-39	49		
Col. 4:10 (NASB)			
Philem. 23-24	61		
2 Tim. 4:11	67		
1 Pet. 5:13	68		

tween his turning back at Perga (Acts 13:13) and his writing of the gospel at Rome some twenty years later? Blaiklock comments on this, "He was taking up the task he abandoned at Perga. . . . In Mark's Gospel . . . we meet the man who failed and tried again, the man who, by a friend's help, rebuilt a testimony, and left that testimony in a deathless book."[5] What lessons can Christians learn from this?

4. *Mark's character.* A character sketch of Mark based on the Bible is at best only partial. But from the verses about him, and the gospel written by him, there emerges a portrait of an energetic servant of Christ who was impulsive, hasty, alert, zealous, friendly, cooperative, humble, and honest. Mark matured over the years, just as his spiritual father, Peter, did. At the peak of that divine process he had the intense joy of penning the "unadorned and unpretentious, but quite overpowering"[6] gospel according to Mark.

5. *Death.* Mark died not long after Peter's martyrdom of A.D. 67, according to tradition.

B. The Book of Mark

1. *Title.* A common title appearing in ancient Greek manuscripts of Mark is *Euaggelion kata Markon* ("gospel according to Mark"). The account is the "gospel of Jesus Christ" (1:1), *according to* the divinely inspired writer, Mark.

2. *Place and date of writing.* Mark wrote his book while living in Rome. There are two main views as to the date of writing:

---

4. For the places involved in some of the passages, follow the views that Paul wrote Colossians from Rome; "Babylon" was a symbolical reference to Rome; and Timothy was living at Ephesus when Paul wrote 2 Timothy.
5. Blaiklock, pp. 14-15.
6. C. F. D. Moule, *The Gospel According to Mark*, p. 4.

early, and late.[7] This manual follows the latter view that the gospel was finished around A.D. 68, soon after Peter's death and before the fall of Jerusalem (A.D. 70).[8] According to this view, Matthew and Luke had already been written.

3. *Peter's contribution.* Some time near the close of the earthly lives of Peter and Paul, a gospel record of the ministry of Jesus was taking shape in the mind of Mark, by the moving of the Holy Spirit. At the time, both Mark and Peter were living in Rome. Mark's gospel was to be a brief eyewitness account of Jesus' life. But Mark, not being one of the twelve apostles of Jesus, obviously did not see or hear firsthand much of Jesus' ministry. This is where Peter came into the picture. Peter's close relationship with Jesus, as one of His apostles, fitted him superbly for sharing with Mark the eyewitness data for writing. We may wonder why Peter, a gifted writer, was not chosen to write the gospel. We are satisfied that God knew what kind of a gospel record He wanted and that Mark was the person so fitted for the task. So it was Peter the informant, Mark the writer, and God the inspirer.

4. *Purpose.* Mark's gospel was especially directed to the Roman mind,[9] which was impressed more by action and power than by discourse and dialogue. Hence it would be accurate to say that Mark stressed "the actions, not so much the words, of Jesus," to reach such an audience with the claims of the gospel. Chart A shows a few of Mark's distinctive features compared with those of the other three gospels.

COMPARISON OF THE FOUR GOSPELS   Chart A

	MATTHEW	MARK	LUKE	JOHN
Jesus as:	King of Israel	Servant of the Lord	Son of Man	Son of God
Reader:	Jew	Roman	Greek	World
Prominent ideas:	Law and Promise	Power and Service	Grace and Fellowship	Glory and Life

Chart B shows the coverage that Mark gives to the public ministry of Christ (the shaded areas represent Mark's coverage). Such selectivity is always divinely inspired. How many chapters of Mark are devoted to the extended ministries of the second year of Jesus'

7. For a defense of an early date of A.D. 50, see W. Graham Scroggie, *A Guide to the Gospels* (London: Pickering & Inglis, 1948), pp. 170-71.
8. Mark had prophesied the city's fall in chap. 13 of his gospel.
9. Among evidences of a non-Jewish audience is the fact that Mark explains Jewish and Aramaic terms and customs not clear to the average Roman (e.g., in 5:41; 7:2-4, 11, 34).

public ministry? Compare this with the number of chapters devoted to the last week—the period of sacrifice.

5. *Theme.* A key verse of Mark identifies clearly the theme of Mark's gospel: "For even the Son of man came not to be ministered unto, but to minister, and to give his life a ransom for many" (10:45). We will look more into this subject in our survey study of Lesson 2.

Some Review Questions

See how much of this lesson you can recall by answering the following questions:

1. What was Mark's home background?

2. When was Mark born, and how old was he when he died?

3. What were the highlights of Mark's Christian service?

4. How did each of the following men influence Mark's life: Barnabas, Paul, Peter?

5. What kind of a person was Mark?

6. Some believe that Mark was the first gospel to be written, partly because it is the shortest of the four gospels. How might you account for its brevity if it was written at the late date of A.D. 68, *after* Matthew and Luke had already been written?

7. Why did God want more than one gospel account written, rather than one large composite work?

8. What is the purpose and theme of Mark's gospel?

9. List some spiritual lessons you have learned in your study thus far.

THE LIFE OF CHRIST SHOWING COVERAGE BY MARK (Shaded area)

Chart B

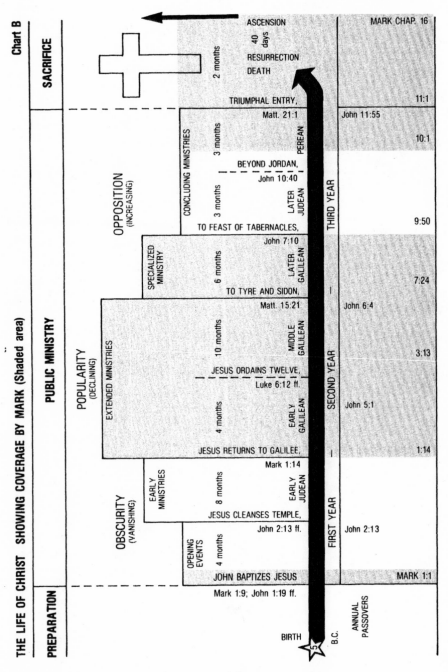

| PREPARATION | PUBLIC MINISTRY | | | SACRIFICE |

OBSCURITY (VANISHING)
POPULARITY (DECLINING)
OPPOSITION (INCREASING)

OPENING EVENTS
EARLY MINISTRIES
EXTENDED MINISTRIES
SPECIALIZED MINISTRY
CONCLUDING MINISTRIES

ASCENSION
40 days
RESURRECTION
DEATH
2 months

MARK CHAP. 16

TRIUMPHAL ENTRY,
Matt. 21:1

11:1

John 11:55

3 months
PEREAN
10:1

BEYOND JORDAN,
John 10:40

3 months
LATER JUDEAN

THIRD YEAR

TO FEAST OF TABERNACLES,
John 7:10

9:50

6 months
LATER GALILEAN

7:24

TO TYRE AND SIDON,
Matt. 15:21

John 6:4

10 months
MIDDLE GALILEAN

SECOND YEAR

3:13

JESUS ORDAINS TWELVE,
Luke 6:12 ff.

John 5:1

4 months
EARLY GALILEAN

JESUS RETURNS TO GALILEE,
Mark 1:14

1:14

8 months
EARLY JUDEAN

FIRST YEAR

JESUS CLEANSES TEMPLE,
John 2:13 ff.

John 2:13

4 months

JOHN BAPTIZES JESUS

MARK 1:1

Mark 1:9; John 1:19 ff.

BIRTH
5
B.C.

ANNUAL PASSOVERS

14

Lesson 2
Survey

With this lesson we begin our study of the actual text of Mark's gospel. Our task here is to survey the whole book, mainly for general impressions, before moving on to analyze each smaller part. "Image the whole, then execute the parts" is the standard procedure.

Your survey study of Mark will be both stimulating and fruitful if you know WHAT you are searching for and HOW to do the searching. Four main activities constitute the WHAT of survey study:

1. Discovering the book's overall *theme*
2. Observing *patterns* and *movements* in the literary structure, or organization, of the book
3. Noting *highlights* of the book and finding *clues* for the study of its various parts
4. Getting a *feel* for the book's atmosphere and approach

Keep these goals always before you as you make your survey study of Mark.

As to the HOW (method) of survey study, there are various procedures. Basically, however, survey study is of three main stages: (1) making the initial acquaintance of the book; (2) scanning the prominent individual items; and (3) searching for the integrating relationships. These are the things we will be doing for the remainder of this lesson. An important bit of advice here is that throughout your survey study of this lesson you avoid getting bogged down in small details. Keep in mind that detailed analysis begins with Lesson 3.

I. STAGE ONE: MAKING THE INITIAL ACQUAINTANCE

1. Scan the book of Mark in one sitting if possible. It is not necessary to read every word or line at this time. If your Bible has

paragraph divisions, reading the first sentence of each paragraph will suffice for now. If your Bible has chapter or paragraph headings, note these as you scan the book.

2. Write down your first impressions.

3. What is the atmosphere of the book as a whole?

4. List any key words and phrases that stand out as of this reading.

II. STAGE TWO: SCANNING INDIVIDUAL ITEMS

1. First let us identify the sequence of segments in Mark that we will follow throughout this manual. (A segment is a group of paragraphs that represent a unit of study. A segment may be longer or shorter than a chapter.)[1] Twenty segments are laid out on Chart C. Mark in your Bible the beginning of each segment, as an aid for the studies that follow.

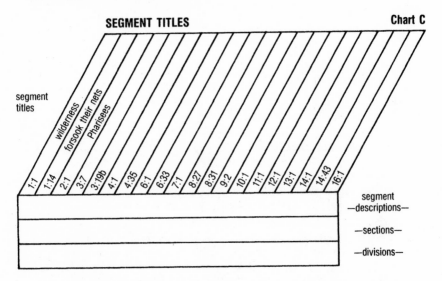

2. Now scan the book of Mark again, segment by segment. Assign a segment title to each unit. (A segment title is a strong word or short phrase, preferably taken from the text, intended to serve as a clue to at least one main part of the segment.) Record these on Chart C (examples are given). The value of this step of survey

1. The nomenclature used in this manual is the following: a segment is a group of paragraphs; a section is a group of segments, and a division is a group of sections.

is not in the segment title itself but in the mental process of beginning to identify parts and movements of the book.

3. What other things have you observed about Mark, in addition to your first impression? Make a list of these. Compare your observations with this partial list:

a. Most of the different actions in Mark are short—like candid snapshots.

b. Most of the text reports events, with little comment.

c. Some of the most awesome and soul-shaking events are recorded in what appears to be calm, matter-of-fact fashion.

d. The word "immediately" appears often.

e. The narrative does not report the birth and infancy of Jesus.

f. Although most of the gospel is narrative, two long teaching sections appear in 4:1-34 (parables) and chapter 13 (prophecy).[2]

g. Mark frequently reports personal gestures of Jesus (e.g., 3:5; 5:41; 7:33; 8:23; 9:27; 10:16); emotions of Jesus (3:5; 6:6, 34; 8:12; 10:14, 21); and people's reactions to Jesus' ministries (1:27; 2:7; 4:41; 6:14; 7:37; 14:1).

4. The writing style of Mark can be described as graphic, vigorous, concise, clear, orderly, and dynamic. Can you think of different examples from the text that illustrate these descriptions?

III. STAGE THREE: LOOKING FOR INTEGRATING RELATIONSHIPS

Mark, like the other three gospels, is a unified story of selected parts of Jesus' life. Let us see how the author organized his material.

A. Looking for a key turning point in the narrative

It is clear from all four gospels that Jesus came to this earth to minister by *life* and by *death*. Mark 10:45, which we shall use as a key verse for Mark, states this clearly. (Read the verse.) Where in Mark's gospel does Jesus move from the *ministration* phase to the *sacrifice* phase by explicitly telling of His coming death? The answer is: at 8:27ff. (Read these verses). Survey Chart D shows 8:27-30 as the strategic center of Mark, with a main division at 8:31. (Study carefully this part of Chart C.)

Observe the key question of Jesus, and Peter's answer, in 8:27-30. Then study the following diagram, which is a key outline for Mark's gospel:

2. A comparison of the four gospels shows these percentages reporting Christ's words: Mark, 43 percent; Luke and John, nearly 50 percent; and Matthew, 60 percent.

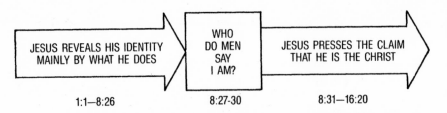

JESUS REVEALS HIS IDENTITY MAINLY BY WHAT HE DOES	WHO DO MEN SAY I AM?	JESUS PRESSES THE CLAIM THAT HE IS THE CHRIST
1:1—8:26	8:27-30	8:31—16:20

Up to 8:27, Mark shows how Jesus revealed His true identity mainly by His deeds. Then (8:27-30), Jesus inquires about His reputation. People have not seen Him as the Son of God but only as one sent from God (such as John the Baptist or Elijah). To extend His public ministry by giving more of the same kind of revelation would not change the people's reactions. He has basically fulfilled His task of ministering ("For even the Son of man came . . . to minister," 10:45*a*) and must now proceed to the second task, that of giving His life ("and to give his life a ransom for many," 10:45*b*). This was not the life of a mere man but of the Christ—the anointed (*krino*) Messiah—whom Peter, by revelation, confessed Him to be (8:29). And so, as 8:31 records, Jesus begins to teach His disciples *explicitly* that He must suffer, be rejected, be killed, and after three days rise again. The story of Mark from this point on, then, is the story of *sacrifice*.

B. Looking for groups of material

An effective way of showing the skeletal framework of Mark is to construct a survey chart similar to Chart D. The bulk of a survey chart shows how the small individual segments combine to make groups of material with a common subject. For example, the two segments beginning at 14:1 and 14:43 are identified as the section, JESUS AS SACRIFICE (see survey chart).

One of the advantages of a survey chart over a standard outline is that various topical outlines can be viewed simultaneously. Also a survey chart is a vivid eye-gate reference for context as one analyzes an individual segment. A division, which is a group of sections, is determined in the same manner as a section. Study the divisions shown on Chart D.

You may want to construct your own survey chart by looking for groups of subject matter similar to the example given above. In any case, study Chart D carefully before proceeding with the next lesson, for such an overview of the book of Mark will help you immeasurably as you proceed with your analytical studies.

Observe the following on this survey chart:

1. Compare the opening segment and the concluding segment.
2. What outlines show two main divisions in the book?
3. Study the various sectional and divisional outlines.
4. Note the geographical pattern of Mark's account.
5. Record at the bottom of the chart the various oppositions to Jesus and the part the disciples play in the gospel record. (You may want to do this exercise as you move along in the study guide.)

C. Identifying a main theme

In your own words, what is the main theme of Mark? Your survey study up to this point should supply the answer. Try also assigning a title to Mark that would coincide with the theme. Observe the title shown on Chart D, "The Servant Jesus."

A *Summary of Mark's Gospel*

Keep Chart D before you as you read the following summary, observing the swift movement of action in Mark's gospel:

> Announced and anointed for a redemptive ministry (Presentation 1:1-13), Jesus preached and worked in the company of the multitudes, attracting many (Popularity 1:14-45) and angering not a few (Opposition 2:1–3:6). Jesus anticipated the day when He would no longer minister on this earth; therefore He began to organize a band of close disciples. (Organization 3:7-35) while He continued to teach (Parables 4:1-34) and perform miracles (Miracles 4:36–5:43). Delegating more and more responsibility to the disciples (6:1-32), He nevertheless remained the tireless servant of the multitudes, constantly revealing His true identity but eventually coming to the moment when this phase of His ministry concluded (Peak of Advance 6:33–8:30). From this point on, as He set His face toward Jerusalem for the last time, He pressed the claim of His being the Christ. He explicitly told of His coming death and resurrection (Jesus as Redeemer 8:31–10:52), and claimed divine authority and prophesied of the future (Jesus as Lord 11:1–13:37). Now the death plot is drawn up (Plot 14:1-11); Jesus spends His last hours of fellowship with His disciples (With Disciples 14:12-42); and He is tried, crucified, and buried (14:43–15:47). Raised from the dead by God, He appears to His disciples and gives them the mandate of worldwide evangelization, as He is received up into heaven (Triumph chap. 16).

MARK THE SERVANT JESUS

Chart D

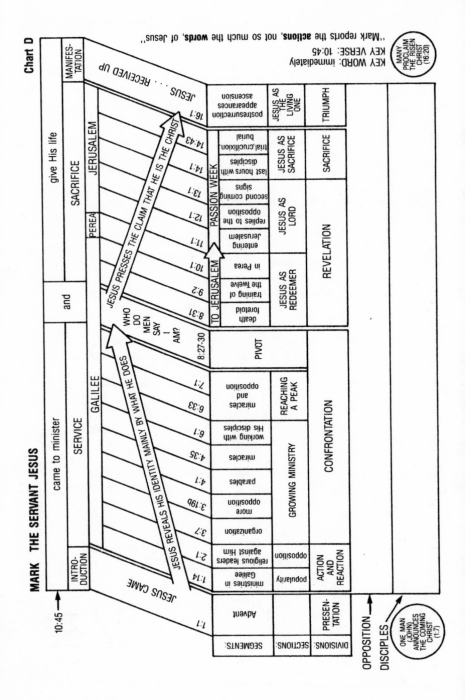

"Mark reports the **actions**, not so much the **words**, of Jesus."

KEY WORD: immediately
KEY VERSE: 10:45

MANY PROCLAIM THE RISEN CHRIST (16:20)

ONE MAN (JOHN) ANNOUNCES THE COMING CHRIST (1:7)

20

Lesson 3

Jesus Came

From this point on in our study of Mark we shall be analyzing in detail the text of the gospel. The segment of this lesson illustrates Mark's concise style: in thirteen opening verses he brings his reader up to that point in Jesus' adult life (age about thirty) when He launched out on His public ministry, a ministry that would last three brief but full years.

I. PREPARATION FOR STUDY

1. Read the Old Testament passages that Mark quotes in 1:2-3: Malachi 3:1*a* (cf. Ex. 23:20); Isaiah 40:3.

2. Read these prophecies of the baptizing ministry of the Holy Spirit in the New Testament age: Isaiah 44:3; Ezekiel 36:26-27; Joel 2:28-32. Also read Acts 1:5; 2:4, 16-21.

3. John the Baptist[1] was the New Testament counterpart of Elijah (Mark 9:13; cf. Matt. 17:12-13). Read 2 Kings 1:8, and note some resemblances of Elijah to John.

4. Review survey Chart D, to see the context of the passage of this lesson.

5. For a more accurate translation of the Greek reading of Mark 1:4, note this change in your Bible: Instead of "John did baptize . . . preach," render "John came, baptizing . . . .preaching." Also, end verse 1 with a period and verse 3 with a comma. The significance of these changes will be evident when you analyze the text later.

6. Decide now how you will want to record your analytical studies from lesson to lesson. The suggestion of this manual is that in addition to a plain sheet of notebook paper for recording *miscellaneous* observations, you have a work sheet (standard size

---

1. Some prefer to call this forerunner of Jesus "John the Baptizer."

8 1/2" x 11") for an *organized* recording of your studies. On this work sheet draw a rectangle (4" x 9") similar to that of Chart E, marked off in paragraph boxes. Use the space inside each box for recording key words and phrases of the Bible text, and the space in the margins for observations and outlines stated briefly in your own words. This is what is called an analytical chart. Examples of such recorded observations will appear from time to time throughout the manual.[2] It is important that you establish right from the start the habit of *recording your observations,* whatever method you use. Record even when the manual does not give explicit directions to do so.

II. ANALYSIS

Segment to be analyzed: 1:1-13
Paragraph divisions: at verses 1, 2, 9, 12 (mark these in your Bible now)

A. General Analysis

1. Read the segment once or twice, underlining key words and phrases in your Bible as you read. Record these on Chart E.
2. What is the main subject of each paragraph? (Record.) What is the main theme of the segment?

_____

_____

Choose a phrase from the segment that could be called a key text for this theme.

_____

_____

3. Who are the main characters of the passage?

_____

_____

Who is the *key* person?

_____

_____

Make a study of Jesus as the object of action in each paragraph. (Compare your study with that shown on Chart E.)

2. For a thorough description of the analytical chart method, consult my *Independent Bible Study.*

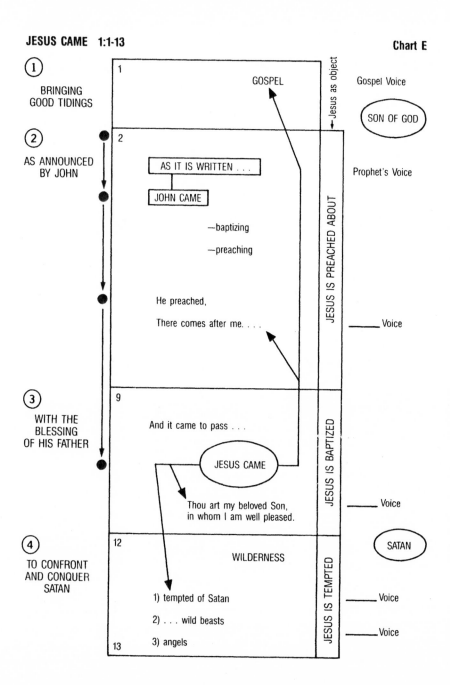

① **BRINGING GOOD TIDINGS**

GOSPEL — Gospel Voice

SON OF GOD

Jesus as object — Jesus as object

② **AS ANNOUNCED BY JOHN**

AS IT IS WRITTEN . . .

JOHN CAME

—baptizing

—preaching

He preached,

There comes after me. . . .

Prophet's Voice

Voice

JESUS IS PREACHED ABOUT

③ **WITH THE BLESSING OF HIS FATHER**

And it came to pass . . .

JESUS CAME

Thou art my beloved Son, in whom I am well pleased.

JESUS IS BAPTIZED

Voice

④ **TO CONFRONT AND CONQUER SATAN**

WILDERNESS

1) tempted of Satan

2) . . . wild beasts

3) angels

JESUS IS TEMPTED

SATAN

Voice

Voice

4. What references to the three Persons of the Trinity do you see in the passage?

_____

_____

5. Compare the first paragraph with the last.
6. Where is the deity of Christ taught in the segment?

_____

7. Complete the study of *voices*, shown on Chart E.

B. Paragraph Analysis

1. *Paragraph 1:1.* How many strong words appear in this introductory statement?

_____

_____

List various truths taught by each word.

_____

_____

Compare "beginning" with the concepts of continuation and culmination. What does the word "gospel" mean literally?[3]

_____

_____

Compare these references to "gospel" in Mark 1:1, 14, 15; 8:35; 10:29; 13:10; 14:9; 16:15. What truths do the titles "Christ" and "Son of God" add to the name "Jesus"? (On "Jesus," read Matt. 1:21.)

_____

_____

With the help of a concordance compare how often this name and the two titles appear in Mark.
2. *Paragraph 1:2-8.* Using the small changes of reading suggested earlier, observe the main core[4] of verses 2-4 as being "John

---

3. Word studies can be an exciting part of your Bible study. Two excellent sources for help in this are: an exhaustive concordance (such as Strong's or Young's) and W.E. Vine, *An Expository Dictionary of New Testament Words* (Westwood, N.J.: Revell, 1961).
4. The main core of a sentence is the combination of main subject, main verb and main object.

came." "As it is written . . . *John came.*" What does this teach about Old Testament prophecy?

_____

_____

Now observe that later in the paragraph John makes a prophecy. What is it?

_____

_____

Where in the segment is this prophecy fulfilled?

_____

Compare the two statements "John came" and "Jesus came." Which is the prominent one? How does Mark show it to be prominent?

_____

_____

Compare the *message* of John's preaching (1:4) and the *person* of his preaching (1:7).

_____

_____

When John baptized a person, what did this rite signify?

_____

_____

How did this ministry fulfill the prophecies that he would "prepare" the way for Jesus' coming (1:2) and "make his paths straight" (1:3)?

_____

_____

Did John expect Jesus to ask to be baptized of him? (Cf. Matt. 3:13-15.)

_____

_____

Why do you think verse 6 was included in this passage?

_____

How does Mark compare John's baptizing ministry with Jesus'?
zl1p6

_____

_____

3. *Paragraph 1:9-11.* Relate the key center, "Jesus came," to the key verse of Mark 10:45).

_____

Contrast Mark's reference to Nazareth (in view of John 1:46) with the last words of the paragraph.

_____

How many words does Mark devote to Jesus' being baptized by John? Compare this with Matthew 3:13-15 and Luke 3:21.

_____

According to 1:10-11, what things did Jesus see and hear after His baptism?

_____

How did each relate to His imminent public ministry?

_____

On the Father's words of 1:11, compare Isaiah 42:1-2.

4. *Paragraph 1:12-13.* The word "driveth" of verse 12 is the same word used of Jesus' *casting out* demons (e.g., Matt. 1:34) and His *driving out* the Temple abusers (John 2:15). Why is such a strong word used in Mark 1:12 to describe this experience of Jesus?

_____

_____

What various truths of Jesus' wilderness trial are taught by 1:13?

Mark does not record the outcome of Jesus' wilderness temptations as do Matthew and Luke. Is the outcome implied?

Why was such an experience vital for Jesus at the *beginning* of His public ministry?

Compare the phrase "tempted of Satan" (1:13) with "preaching the gospel" in the next verse (1:14).

III. NOTES

1. *"Gospel" (1:1)*. This word translates the Greek *evangelion* (*eu*, "good," plus *aggelion*, "message"). It has been observed that in classical Greek the word first meant a reward given to the bearers of good news; that it subsequently came to mean the sacrifice offered in thankfulness for good news; until finally it was used of the good news itself (this being the New Testament usage).[5]

2. *"Make his paths straight" (1:3)*. The picture is that of clearing a highway for the anticipated procession of an important figure, such as a king. This was John's spiritual ministry, to help clear away obstacles in the hearts of people so that when Jesus came they would acknowledge who He was and listen to His voice.

3. "Repentance" (1:4). The word means more than a state of mind, in grief and sorrow. It has the responsive connotation of change of conduct, direction, purpose.

4. *"Holy Ghost" (1:8)*. "Ghost" is a King James Version word for "Spirit."

5. *"Like a dove" (1:10)*. Luke adds the description "in a bodily shape" (Luke 3:22). In no other place in the Bible does the Spirit appear in the form of a dove. The docile character of the dove (Matt. 10:16) has made it a symbol of peace. The dove was also an

5. See G. Campbell Morgan, *The Gospel According to Mark*, p. 12.

Old Testament sacrifice of the poorest of offerers (Lev. 12:8; Luke 2:24).

IV. FOR THOUGHT AND DISCUSSION

1. What is the meaning of "remission of sins" (1:4)? How is this work related to man's repentance? How is repentance related to saving faith?

2. What is the purpose of church ordinances and rites, such as water baptism?

3. When did Jesus begin to fulfill John's prophecy that He would baptize people with the Holy Spirit? What constitutes this divine work? (Cf. Luke 24:49; Acts 1:8; 2:1-22.)

4. Why was Jesus baptized? Consider this threefold answer: (1) as the fulfillment of all righteousness (Matt. 3:15); (2) as an identification with mankind (without participating in their sin) (Isa. 53:12); (3) as an act of dedication to the ministry of accomplishing His Father's will (cf. John 5:30).

5. What spiritual truths are suggested by the symbol of the dove descending upon Jesus (1:10)? What does this teach about Christian service?

6. What were Jesus' wilderness temptations? (Cf. Matt. 4:1-11 and Luke 4:1-13.) What is the difference between temptation and sin? Study Hebrews 2:18; 4:15; 1 Corinthians 10:13. Which is more difficult, to yield to temptation or to turn away from it victoriously? What was Jesus' experience?

7. Think about the relationships of each of these three key experiences of Jesus:

   a. His baptism—wherein He identified Himself with man

   b. His anointing—wherein He was accredited by God

   c. His temptation—wherein He conquered the arch-enemy, Satan

8. Make a list of five to ten important spiritual lessons taught by Mark 1:1-13. If you are studying in a group, discuss ways to apply these lessons in daily life. Always be specific in your applications.

V. FURTHER STUDY

Three subjects suggested for further word study and doctrinal study are repentance, water and spirit baptism, and temptation.

VI. WORDS TO PONDER

The gospel of Jesus (1:1).

Of the name "Jesus" G. Campbell Morgan writes, "That is the name that places Him upon the level of my comprehension. . . . Take Him away from me, and I am lost. . . . The charm of this gospel is that through it we shall be following Jesus, walking with him, watching. . . ."[6]

6. Ibid., p. 14.

Lesson 4

Mark 1:14-15

Jesus' Fame

The first year of Jesus' ministry is called the year of obscurity, for His fame was confined to Judea. In Mark's gospel this year of obscurity is located between 1:13 and 1:14, so that the action of this lesson took place about a year after that of Lesson 3.[1] One of the brightest phrases in this passage is the concluding one, "and they came to him from every quarter" (1:45). Jesus' fame would shortly vanish like vapor, but even His foreknowledge of that could not have dispelled His joy at seeing the multitudes flock after Him at this time.

I. PREPARATION FOR STUDY

1. Refer back to Chart B and observe where Mark 1:14 is located in the story of Jesus' life. Note the year of obscurity between 1:13 and 1:14.

2. Note the context of this lesson's passage (1:14-45) on the survey Chart D.

3. Have a mental picture of the location of Galilee in relation to Jerusalem (see map).

4. Keep in mind this part of the key outline of Mark:

JESUS REVEALS HIS IDENTITY MAINLY BY WHAT HE DOES

"WHO DO MEN SAY THAT I AM?"

1:1—8:26   8:27-30

1. Most of Jesus' early Judean ministries are reported only in John's gospel (John 1:19–4:42).

30

II. ANALYSIS

Segment to be analyzed: 1:14-15
Paragraph divisions: at verses 14, 16, 21, 29, 32, 35, 40

A. General Analysis

1. After you have marked the paragraph divisions in your Bible, read the passage paragraph by paragraph. Underline key words and phrases. Record paragraph titles on Chart F.

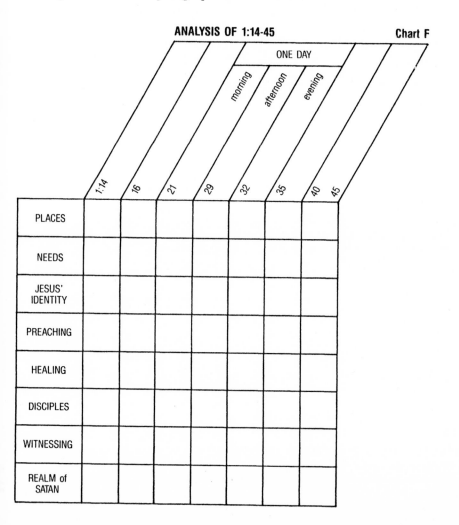

ANALYSIS OF 1:14-45

Chart F

ONE DAY — morning, afternoon, evening

	1:14	16	21	29	32	35	40	45
PLACES								
NEEDS								
JESUS' IDENTITY								
PREACHING								
HEALING								
DISCIPLES								
WITNESSING								
REALM of SATAN								

2. What parts of this account strike you?

_____

_____

What have you seen for the first time?

_____

_____

3. Compare the references to "came" in the first verse of the segment (1:14) and the last (1:45). What spiritual lessons can be
learned from this?

_____

_____

_____

4. Eight subjects are listed on Chart F. Read the passage more
slowly, recording under each paragraph what it reports about the
subjects. You will observe many interesting things in this study.

B. Paragraph Analysis

1. *Paragraph 1:14-15.* What contrast do you observe in verse 14?

_____

_____

Analyze the different parts of Jesus' message (v. 15).

_____

_____

What does He mean by "the kingdom of God is at hand"? (Cf. John
3:3, 5; Col. 1:13.)

_____

_____

What two commands does He give? How are they related?

_____

_____

2. *Paragraph 1:16-20.* What is the key verse of this paragraph?

_____

_____

Observe Jesus' parabolic method of talking about spiritual truths (v. 17) in the language of everyday affairs and material things. He said to Simon and Andrew, who were fishing at the time, "I will make you fishers of men." What then may He have said to James and John, who were mending nets at the time (v. 19)?

Note what Mark says Simon and Andrew forsook (v. 18), and what James and John forsook (v. 20).

What spiritual truths are taught by the three verbs of verse 20?

3. *Paragraph 1:21-28.* What ministries of Jesus bring about the result of verse 28?

What do verses 22 and 27 reveal about Jesus' doctrine?

How would Jesus' teaching differ from that of the scribes?

Explain the interchange of singular and plural pronouns in the story of the unclean spirit (1:23-27).

How do you account for the fact that the demonic world knows and acknowledges who Jesus is (1:24)?

4. *Paragraph 1:29-31.* In what ways was this a timely experience for the four disciples and their families?

_____

5. *Paragraph 1:32-34.* Note the repetition of "all" and "many." Explain Jesus' reason for not allowing the demons to speak about Him (1:34).

_____

6. *Paragraph 1:35-39.* Why did Jesus need to pray?

_____

Why did He choose this time of day and place (1:35)?

_____

Explain Jesus' reason for moving away from the multitudes of 1:37.

_____

7. *Paragraph 1:40-45.* What does this paragraph teach about:
the heart of Jesus:

_____

the power of Jesus:

_____

the wisdom of Jesus:

_____

the popularity of Jesus:

_____

Account for His instructions to the healed leper (1:44). (Read Lev. 13:1-3; 14:1 ff.)

_____

_____

How did Jesus view the law of Moses? (Cf. Matt. 5:17.)

Compare Jesus' withdrawal to the desert by "force" (1:45) with His withdrawal to the desert by choice (1:35).

III. NOTES

1. *"Kingdom of God" (1:15).* The reference here is to God's present spiritual reign in the hearts of men.

2. *"He saw Simon and Andrew" (1:16).* This was not Jesus' first contact with these men. Read John 1:35-42. Also, the John of Mark 1:19 may have been one of the two disciples referred to in John 1:35.

3. *"Entered into the synagogue, and taught" (1:21).* "It was the custom for the President of the synagogue . . . to arrange who should read and expound the Scriptures each sabbath, and at this stage of His ministry this provided Jesus with manifold opportunities, for wherever He went He would be invited to teach."[2] The synagogue service consisted or prayer, praise, reading of Scripture, and exposition by a rabbi or another person with the credentials of a teacher.

Morgan makes this interesting observation concerning the synagogue buildings of Jesus' time:

> These synagogues usually faced the west, not only because, according to Ezekiel's prophecy, there was a danger of idolatry in turning to the east, but also symbolically they were thus taught not to look in worship toward the place from whence religion came, but toward the place to which religion was intended to reach. It was the missionary attitude.[3]

4. *"Taught them as one that had authority" (1:22).* "It was not the authority of the law, it was not the authority of a manner, it was the authority of naked, eternal truth, uttered through an absolutely perfect man."[4]

2. F. Davidson, et al., *The New Bible Commentary*, p. 810.
3. G. Campbell Morgan, *The Gospel According to Mark*, p. 35.
4. Ibid., p. 36.

5. *"Devils" (1:32).* The Greek word is correctly translated "demons." There are legions of demons, but only one devil (Satan; Rev. 12:9).

6. *Jesus "suffered not the devils [demons] to speak" (1:34).* The demons are agents of Satan, the devil. Christ did not want them to have any part in the propagation of the gospel, which involves telling the world who Jesus really is. As G. Campbell Morgan says, "Admit the devil into the fellowship of this propaganda of the Gospel, and ere long he will twist his fingers round the Gospel and distort it, until it becomes a deadly and damnable heresy."[5]

IV. FOR THOUGHT AND DISCUSSION

1. Jesus preached repentance and faith as conditions for entrance into God's kingdom. Why are these necessary for a person's salvation? As you move along in the gospel of Mark, look for other things said by Jesus about the way of salvation (e.g., 2:5, 14; 3:35).

2. Why did Christ seek out a select group of disciples early in His public ministry? How are Christians today involved in the call and commission to discipleship? What price must Christians be willing to pay for this privilege and responsibility?

3. "The antidote for the pressure of a busy Christian life is prayer." Can this application be made from 1:35 and 1:45? If Christ needed to pray to His Father, how much more do we? What may be said about time, place, and attitudes of prayer?

4. Study this comment concerning the healed leper: "Having first experienced the power of Christ, the man is then able to fulfill the requirements of the law."[6] What is the Christian's relation to the law of God?

5. What are some important applications to your personal life based on truths taught in the passage for this lesson?

V. FURTHER STUDY

Inquire more into what the New Testament teaches about these subjects:

1. the kingdom of God
2. demonism[7]

---

5. Morgan, *The Parables and Metaphors of Our Lord*, p. 385.
6. Davidson, p. 811.
7. A recommended source book on demonism is Merrill F. Unger, *Biblical Demonology* (Wheaton, Ill.: Van Kampen, 1952).

3. The Christian and God's law, according to the epistle to the Galatians.

VI. WORDS TO PONDER

Come ye after me, and I WILL MAKE YOU TO BECOME . . . (1:17).

Lesson 5

Hostility Sets In

Soon Jesus' popularity with the masses was marred by stinging accusations from the religionists. It is interesting to observe from
the gospels that the first open challenge by the Jewish religious
leaders was made when Jesus talked about sin and claimed divine
authority to forgive sin. They had earlier accepted Him as a prophet of God, performing great wonders, but now, as far as they were
concerned, He was meddling and presuming too much. This is
the story of our present lesson.

I. PREPARATION FOR STUDY

1. Refer to a Bible dictionary or Bible encyclopedia for descriptions of these groups: Pharisees, Herodians, scribes.
2. Read the following passages as background to the accusations that Jesus and His disciples were breaking the Mosaic law:
Leviticus 16:29; 23:27; Numbers 29:7; Deuteronomy 23:25; Exodus
20:10; 34:21; Leviticus 24:9; 1 Samuel 21:1-6.
3. Locate Capernaum on the map. What features would make
this a good home base for Jesus' Galilean ministry?
4. Prepare a work sheet (such as analytical Chart H) for recording observations.

II. ANALYSIS

Segment to be analyzed: 2:1–3:6
Paragraph divisions: at verses 1, 13, 18, 23; 3:1

A. General Analysis

1. Follow the reading and recording procedures established in the earlier lessons. What is the atmosphere of this passage?

_____

2. Study the progression of accusations appearing in this segment. Record your study on Chart G. What really were the religious leaders objecting to?

_____

_____

THE ACCUSATIONS OF 2:1—3:6 Chart G

	2:1-12	2:13-17	2:18-22	2:23-28	3:1-6
OCCASION AND SETTING					
ACCUSERS					
ACCUSATION					
OBJECT OF ACCUSATION					
SPOKEN TO WHOM					
JESUS' DEFENSE					
PROGRESSION OF OPPOSITION					
RESULT					

What was the climax of their envy and hate, as of this phase of Jesus' ministry?

_____

_____

3. Observe among other things that the charge of 2:1-12 was a theological issue, whereas the remaining charges were over law and tradition (see Chart H).

4. Jesus' answers to the charges were usually based on the principle of *need*. Read through the passage again, observing in each paragraph what Jesus said about this. Compare your study with the outline shown on Chart H. Develop other studies on this work sheet.

B. Paragraph Analysis

1. *Paragraph 2:1-12.* What was the subject of Jesus' preaching (2:2)?

_____

_____

Whose faith did Jesus recognize (2:15)?

_____

_____

Did Jesus imply in His words of 2:5 that the man's paralysis was a direct judgment for sin? (Cf. John 9:2-3; Luke 13:1-5.)

_____

_____

When Jesus spoke the words of verse 5, what do you think was the reaction of the paralytic and of his bearers?

_____

_____

Were the scribes entirely wrong in their reasonings recorded in verse 7?

_____

_____

What does 2:8 reveal about Jesus?

_____

_____

JESUS, THE ANSWER TO MAN'S NEEDS 2:1—3:6

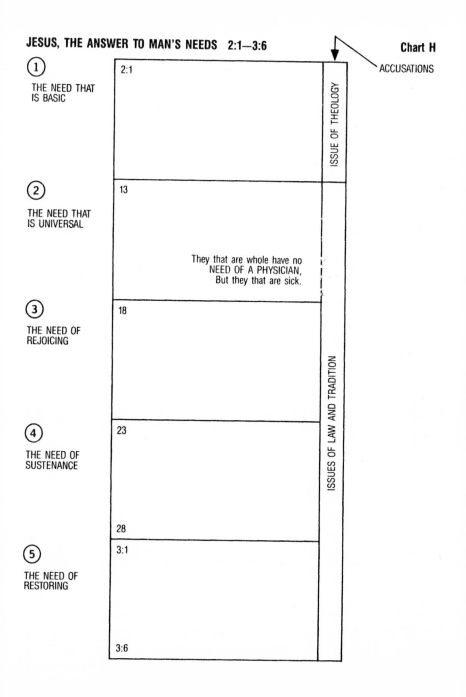

ACCUSATIONS

(1) THE NEED THAT IS BASIC — 2:1

(2) THE NEED THAT IS UNIVERSAL — 13

They that are whole have no
NEED OF A PHYSICIAN,
But they that are sick.

(3) THE NEED OF REJOICING — 18

(4) THE NEED OF SUSTENANCE — 23 ... 28

(5) THE NEED OF RESTORING — 3:1 ... 3:6

ISSUE OF THEOLOGY

ISSUES OF LAW AND TRADITION

What do the first five words of 2:10 reveal about the purpose of Jesus' miracles?

_____

_____

Compare Jesus' references to "Son of Man" in 2:10 to the scribes' reference to "God" in 2:7.

_____

_____

What different characteristics of Jesus are suggested by the title "Son of Man"?

_____

_____

2. *Paragraph 2:13-17*. What do you learn about sovereign calling from 2:14?

_____

_____

What does the occasion of 2:15-16 teach about the risk of misunderstanding?

_____

_____

In your own words, how did Jesus justify His mingling with "publicans and sinners"?

_____

_____

How often do the words "sin" and "sinners" appear in 2:1-17?

_____

_____

What happens to the gospel message when such words are removed from its vocabulary?

_____

_____

3. *Paragraph 2:18-22*. Fast and feast are opposites, associated with sorrow and joy, respectively. What illustrations does Jesus use in answering the challenge of this paragraph?

Note the element of *time* in 2:19-20 and the fact of *unmixables* in 2:21-22. What is Jesus' answer to the charge, in your own words?

---

4. *Paragraph 2:23-28*. The two key statements of Jesus' defense are:
    1. "When he had need" (2:25).
    2. "The sabbath was made for man, and not man for the sabbath" (2:27).
What do these words reveal about Jesus' view of man?

Why did Jesus add the words of verse 28? (*The Living Bible* reads this as, "And I, the Man from Heaven, have authority even to decide what men can do on Sabbath days!")

---

5. *Paragraph 3:1-6*. This is a dramatic conclusion to this phase of Jesus' Galilean tour. Study the sequence:
    "And they watched him" (3:2).
    "But they held their peace" (3:4).
    "And [they] took counsel . . . how they might destroy him" (3:6).
What was the cause of Jesus' anger, in 3:5?

Why would the Pharisees, a Jewish sect, align themselves with their deadliest opponents, the Herodians, a pro-Roman political group?

43

Ponder the intensity of hatred suggested by the words "how they might destroy him" (v. 6). Contrast this with what Jesus had just spoken, in verse 4.

_____

_____

_____

Compare also the ominous foreshadowing of Christ's violent death (3:6) with His own earlier prophecy of 2:20 spoken in milder terms.

_____

_____

With the help of a concordance read other verses in the New Testament where this word "destroy" appears (e.g., Luke 9:56).

III. NOTES

1. _"Son of Man" (2:10)._ Read Daniel 7:13 for what may be the origin of this messianic title. Why do you think this was Jesus' favorite title for Himself?

_____

_____

2. _"Power" (2:10)._ The Greek word is better translated "authority." The full meaning is perhaps the combination of _right_ plus _might_.

3. _"Levi" (2:14)._ Levi's other name was Matthew (Matt. 9:9; Mark 3:18. He may have changed his name to Matthew ("gift of Jehovah") when he became a disciple of Jesus.

4. _"Publicans" (2:15)._ Publicans were tax collectors for Rome in Jesus' day. They were associated with sinners in the phrase "publicans and sinners" because of their notorious reputation for fraud, oppression, and immorality. (Cf. Matt. 18:17; 21:31.)

5. _"Fast" (2:18)._ One fast day a year, the Day of Atonement, was prescribed by the law (Lev. 23:27-29; cf. Acts 27:9). In Jesus' day Pharisees fasted at least twice a week (Luke 18:12).

6. _"Children [literally, "sons"] of the bridechamber" (2:19)._ These were the friends of the bridegroom, who served as his attendants.

7. _"New wine" (2:22)._ Old wineskins would have been stretched to their limit, so that the fermenting of new wine in the "bottles" would burst them. "Thus it is not possible to confine to the struc-

44

ture of the old legalism the vitality of the new experience pro-
duced by faith in Christ."[1]

8. *"Whether he would heal him on the sabbath day" (3:2)*. Rabbinic
tradition permitted the practice of medicine on the Sabbath only if
the patient was on the verge of death.

9. *"Herodians" (3:6)*. These were Jews who favored the rule of
Rome in Palestine. The Pharisees hated all foreign domination.
The one thing they had in common was hatred for Jesus, and here
is where they submerged their differences. The only other reference to the Herodians in the gospels is at Mark 12:13 (and the parallel reference, Matt. 22:16).

IV. FOR THOUGHT AND DISCUSSION

1. What does this passage teach about man, false religion, and
Christ?

2. What have you learned here about Jesus' compassion over
the needs of others?

3. How much compassion is to be found today in the hearts
of people, even of Christians? Mark reports that Jesus was "grieved
for the hardness of their hearts." The word "hardness" could read
"hardening," for the process was going on.[2] *The Living Bible*
makes this vivid paraphrase, "Looking around at them angrily, for
He was deeply disturbed by their *indifference to human need"*
(3:5a).

4. Jesus did not avoid eating and drinking with publicans and
sinners (2:15-17). How do you apply this to Christians today, as to
their responsibility to unsaved people? Consider this diagnosis of
a few decades ago by G. Campbell Morgan:

> I am constrained to say that I believe at this very hour one of
> the . . . reasons for the condition of things in the Christian
> Church that is troubling us in many ways, is the aloofness of the
> Christian Church from sinning men and women. We still build
> our sanctuaries, and set up our standards, and institute our ar-
> rangements, and say to the sinning ones: If you will come to us,
> we will help you! The way of the Lord is to go and sit where they
> sit, without patronage and without contempt.[3]

5. A missionary who had served twenty-three years in the
long grass of Central Africa was asked what impressed him most
forcibly when he returned to London. This was his reply: "The fact

1. C.F. Pfeiffer and E.F. Harrison, eds., *The Wycliffe Bible Commentary*, p. 993.
2. The root of the word translated "hardness" means marblelike stone.
3. G. Campbell Morgan, *The Gospel According to Mark*, p. 61.

that London had lost its smile. I stood on the bridges, and walked along the thoroughfares, and looked at the hurrying peoples, and they all looked so sad." In what ways can you as a Christian convince your unsaved neighbor that the gospel is news of a Saviour bringing *joy,* not *sorrow?*

6. What are the Christians' privileges and obligations in observing the Lord's Day (Sunday)?

V. FURTHER STUDY.

1. Jesus "preached the word unto them" (2:2). Reconstruct what you think may have been the content of, say, a half-hour sermon by Jesus at this time.

2. Make a topical study of "sin" in the New Testament.

3. Trace in the Bible the law of the Sabbath day and the Sabbath principle. Include Isaiah 58:13-14 in your study.

VI. WORDS TO PONDER

Who can forgive sins but God only? (2:7).

The Son of Man has authority on earth to forgive sins (2:10, TEV*).

Today's English Version.

Lesson 6

Mark 3:7–4:34

Ministries to the Disciples and the Multitudes

The decision of the Pharisees and Herodians to destroy Jesus was made halfway through His ministry. It was not God's time for His Son to be slain yet, since His unfinished ministries were many. Mark now reports some of those ministries, selecting highlights of Jesus' Galilean tours, which led up to the peak of this phase of His work. In our survey study we observed how Jesus turned His eyes and feet to Jerusalem for the cross (8:31ff.), after reaching that peak. The progress of Mark's gospel from 3:7 on is shown below:

MINISTRIES OF 3:7—16:20

3:7	6:33	8:27	8:31 16:20	
GROWING MINISTRY	REACHING A PEAK	WHO AM I?	TO JERUSALEM	
Lessons 6-7	Lesson 8	Lessons 9-14		

Observe on the chart that the section GROWING MINISTRY is studied in two lessons (6 and 7). As indicated earlier, you may want to break up each lesson into two or more parts, depending on how much time you can devote to each part.

I. PREPARATION FOR STUDY

1. Review Chart B, observing what part of Jesus' public ministry is covered by the passages of this lesson, 3:7–4:34.

47

2. Keep in mind also that we are studying the chapters of the first half of Mark where "Jesus Reveals His Identity Mainly by What He Does" (Chart D). But as was noted earlier, most of chapter 4 (included in our present lesson) is devoted to Jesus' *word* ministry. Even in a gospel of *action* it is impossible to divorce *words* from *works*.

3. Study the outline on Chart I before you begin to analyze the various parts. Observe that the section called "Growing Ministry" continues into the next chapters (4:35–6:32); and the section called "Ministry in Word" is followed by its counterpart "Ministry in Works" (4:35ff.).

4. Locate on a map the place names of 3:7-8.

II. ANALYSIS

Segments to be analyzed: 3:7-35; and 4:1-34.
Paragraph divisions: at verses 7, 13, 19b,[1] 31; 4:1, 10, 21, 26, 30. (Mark these divisions in your Bible at this time.)

A. General Analysis: Segment 3:7-35

1. Read the segment for initial observations. What are your first impressions?

_____

_____

What is the main point of each paragraph?

_____

_____

Record observations in the boxes of Chart I.
2. Look at the outline of this segment shown on Chart I. How is the first paragraph (3:7-12) introductory to the entire division 3:7–8:30 (called "Confrontation" on survey Chart D)?

_____

_____

What is the bold contrast between this paragraph and the last phrase of 3:6?

_____

_____

1.This division begins with these words: "and they went into a house."

48

3. How is paragraph 3:13-19*a* related to the theme, Growing Ministry?

_____

_____

4. Why do you think Mark included the two paragraphs of 3:19*b*-35?

_____

_____

B. Paragraph Analysis: Segment 3:7-35

1. *Paragraph 3:7-12.* What is the atmosphere of this paragraph? Note the many superlatives (e.g., "great," "many").

_____

Is the paragraph more about Jesus' actions or others' reactions?

_____

What did the multitudes recognize?

_____

What did the unclean spirits recognize?

_____

2. *Paragraph 3:13-19.* Compare the atmosphere of this paragraph with that of the preceding one. Make observations, interpretations, and applications of each of the following strong statements:
    "he . . . calleth unto him whom he would"
    "they came unto him"
    "he ordained twelve"
    "that they should be with him"
    "that he might send them forth"
    "to preach"
    "to have power to heal"
    "to cast out devils"

Chart I

WORK SHEET FOR 3:7—4:34

GROWING MINISTRY →

3:7	3:13	3:19b	3:31	3:35	4:1	4:10	4:21	4:26	4:30	4:34	4:35ff.
SCOPE OF THE MINISTRY	HELPERS IN THE MINISTRY	OPPOSITION TO THE MINISTRY			MINISTRY IN WORD (Parables)						MINISTRY IN WORKS
					THE SOWN SEED		CANDLE AND BUSHEL	SEED AND HARVEST	MUSTARD SEED		

Why did Jesus give surnames to some apostles?[2]

_____

_____

Why does Mark list Judas last?

_____

_____

3. *Paragraph 3:20-30.* The phrase "his friends" translates three words meaning literally "they who were from beside him," that is, by origin or birth. So these no doubt were Jesus' mother and brethren referred to in 3:31-32. What was their concern, and what did they try to do?

_____

_____

In what sense could this be called opposition to Jesus' public ministry?

_____

_____

Compare their thoughts with those of the scribes of 3:22.

_____

_____

How serious was the scribes' charge? Answer this in the light of Mark's comment of verse 30 and Jesus' response of 3:23-29.

_____

_____

4. *Paragraph 3:31-35.* Why did Jesus' mother and brothers want to speak with Him at this time? (3:31-32; cf. v. 21.)

_____

_____

Was Jesus severe in His response of 3:33-35?

_____

_____

_____

2. The name *Simon* means "hearing"; the name *Peter* means "rock."

What truth was He trying to teach at this point in His public ministry?

_____

_____

Compare this with what He had said as a lad to His mother, recorded in Luke 2:49.

_____

_____

C. General Analysis: Segment 4:1-34

1. Read the segment through once, and record the main point of each paragraph on Chart I.
2. What parables are about seed?

_____

_____

What main subject is common to all the parables?

_____

_____

3. Make other general comparisons of the parables.
4. This segment also tells us why Jesus taught in parables. Study carefully verses 10-12 and 33-34,[3] and list reasons for Jesus' parabolic method of teaching the multitudes.

_____

_____

Why was He able to teach the *mysteries* about the kingdom of His disciples (4:11)? Do you think they fully understood those mysteries?

_____

_____

5. Do you think that verse 12 suggests that Jesus used parables to keep the people in spiritual darkness? For the Bible's own com-

---

3. Both of these groups of verses could be set off from the rest of the segment as separate paragraphs.

52

mentary on this verse, read the parallel report in Matthew 13:10-17. Also, read Isaiah 6:9-10, which Matthew paraphrases.

According to Matthew 13:15, who closes whose eyes, and why?

In what way is this a clue to Jesus' use of parables?

What does the last phrase of Mark 4:33 reveal about Jesus' patience?

6. Does the parable of Mark 4:21-25 reveal anything about why Jesus used parables?

D. Paragraph Analysis: Segment 4:1-34

1. Paragraph 4:1-9 and 4:10-20. Study carefully the parallel parts of these paragraphs. Record your observations on Chart I.
2. Paragraph 4:21-25. List various spiritual lessons taught by this parable.

3. Paragraph 4:26-29. What key phrases stand out in this parable?

What is this parable's main teaching concerning the doctrine of the kingdom of God? (The phrase "he knoweth not how" is a clue to this.)

_____

_____

_____

4. Paragraph 4:30-34. This parable is like the one preceding it, but it emphasizes a different aspect of God's kingdom. What is that?

_____

_____

Make a list of the various spiritual lessons taught by the parables of 4:1-34.

_____

_____

_____

_____

III. NOTES

1. *"Beelzebub" (3:22)*. This is a reference to Satan himself, identified in the next phrase of 3:22 as "prince of the demons" (ASV*).

2. *"Hath never forgiveness" (3:29)*. The act of blasphemy against the Holy Spirit comes from an attitude of heart. Of this *The Wycliffe Bible Commentary* writes, "In the light of Scripture as a whole, this attitude can only be a fixed, unrepentant state of mind that persists in defiant rejection of the overtures of the Holy Spirit."[4]

3. *"Asked of him the parable" (4:10)*. Matthew reports that the disciples asked *why* Jesus spoke in parables. Of Jesus' reply in 4:11-12, G. Campbell Morgan comments:

> The method of Christ with rebellious souls who have become gross of heart, dull of hearing, willfully blind, is the hiding of the mysteries which would affright and offend them and the pre-

American Standard Version.

4. C.F. Pfeiffer and E.F. Harrison, eds., *The Wycliffe Bible Commentary*, p. 995. The context of the whole Bible must always be recognized in interpreting difficult passages.

senting of pictures which invite and suggest. If they will answer the invitation of the picture, and follow its suggestion, lo! they will find themselves face to face with the mystery. Therefore the parable is ever an open door to the mystery.[5]

IV. FOR THOUGHT AND DISCUSSION

1. What are different ways today in which the work of the gospel is being opposed and hindered?

2. From your study of 3:13-19a, what are Christ's different ministries in commissioning a Christian worker for His vineyard?

3. Why did Jesus choose Judas Iscariot, even though He knew beforehand that Judas would betray Him?

4. Cite examples of different spiritual "soils" where the gospel is sown today, similar to those described in 4:1-20.

5. Describe the kingdom of God as to the miracle of growth (4:26-29) and the miracle of size (4:30-34).

6. What can Christian teachers learn today from Jesus' parabolic method?

V. FURTHER STUDY

Two interesting subjects for further study are:
1. Jesus' training of the twelve disciples
2. A comparison of the parables of Jesus[6]

VI. WORDS TO PONDER

And be sure to put into practice what you hear. The more you do this, the more you will understand what I tell you (Mark 4:24, TLB*).

*The Living Bible.
5. G. Campbell Morgan, The Gospel According to Mark, pp. 96-97.
6. An excellent book on parables is G. Campbell Morgan's The Parables and Metaphors of Our Lord.

Jesus the Miracle Worker

The main subject of this lesson is Jesus' miracles that He performed while in Galilee. So Jesus' WORDS (parables) of the last lesson are followed by His WORKS (miracles) of this lesson, the latter vindicating the former.

Recall the survey of Mark (Lesson 2) which showed that in 1:1–8:26 Jesus is constantly revealing *who He is* by doing *what He does*. The natural question then which He asks at 8:27-30 is, "Who do men say I am?" This key outline of Mark is diagrammed again at this point in our study because it is so important:

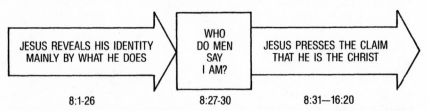

JESUS REVEALS HIS IDENTITY MAINLY BY WHAT HE DOES	WHO DO MEN SAY I AM?	JESUS PRESSES THE CLAIM THAT HE IS THE CHRIST
8:1-26	8:27-30	8:31—16:20

It is interesting to observe that even Jesus' disciples were asking the question, "Who is this?" as they beheld the miracles Jesus was performing in Galilee at this time. (Read 4:41.)

I. PREPARATION FOR STUDY

1. Think more about how important it was for Jesus to show people full credentials as to His identity before He offered Himself as

a sacrifice on the cross. What is the difference between a man dying on a cross[1] and the God-Man dying on the cross of Calvary?

_____

2. Review survey Chart D for the context of the passage of this lesson.
3. Keep in mind that the questions given in each lesson do not cover the entire text of the passage being studied. Look for more things in the text than are suggested by the questions.

II. ANALYSIS

Segment to be analyzed: 4:35–6:32
Paragraph divisions: at verses 4:35; 5:1, 21, 25, 35; 6:1, 6b, 14, 30

A. General Analysis

1. Mark the paragraph divisions in your Bible. Also mark major divisional points at 6:1 and 6:30, as shown on Chart J.
2. Read the passage, marking key words and phrases in your Bible as you read.
3. Think about the general content of this segment. Why is a main division made at 6:1 (as on Chart J)?

_____

How does the last paragraph conclude this part of Mark's account?

_____

4. Record on the work sheet of Chart J your different observations as you study this segment. Begin by recording the different miracles. Observe the outline on *power* shown on the chart.
5. At what points in this passage is the question, "Who is this?" raised? (The question is stated explicitly at one point in the text. Look for other places where it is at least suggested. For example, cf. 6:14 with Luke 9:9.)

_____

_____

_____

1. History records thousands of martyrs crucified thus.

57

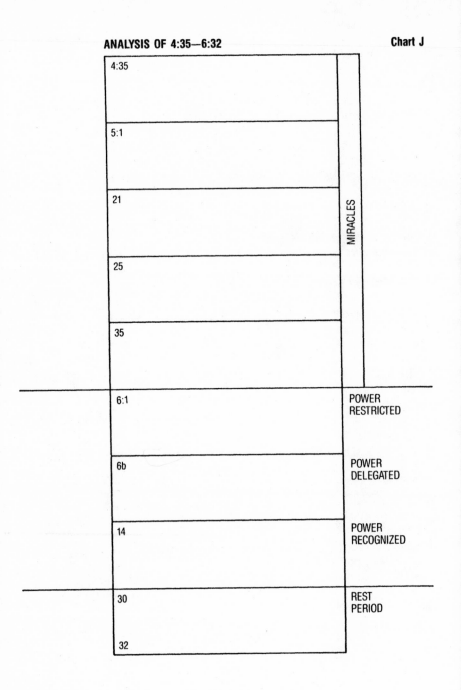

4:35	MIRACLES
5:1	
21	
25	
35	
6:1	POWER RESTRICTED
6b	POWER DELEGATED
14	POWER RECOGNIZED
30	REST PERIOD
32	

6. Make a brief note of the geography of each paragraph, by reading the first verse of each paragraph.

B. Paragraph Analysis

1. *Power over nature (4:35-41).* What do you learn about Jesus from His sleeping during the storm?

_____

_____

Jesus showed power over what two physical elements?

_____

_____

What was the *method* of this miracle?

_____

_____

Explain His words recorded in verse 40.

_____

_____

Compare the storm on the sea with the storm in the hearts of the disciples.

_____

_____

2. *Power over demons (5:1-20).* Compare the turbulence of this setting with that of the preceding paragraph. What important observations do you make in verses 19 and 20?

_____

_____

3. *Power over death (5:21-24 and 5:35-43).* What is the tone of this story?

_____

_____

What was the physical condition of Jairus's daughter as of the first paragraph (5:21-24)?

_____

_____

Observe in paragraph 5:35-43 how quickly Jesus reassured Jairus when news came to him that his daughter had died. What does this reveal about Jesus?

_____

_____

Account for Jesus' first command of 5:43.

_____

_____

4. *Power over disease (5:25-34)*. What kind of faith did the woman have?

_____

_____

Compare this with the faith of the disciples in 4:35-41.

_____

_____

Ponder the truth of Augustine's words "Flesh presses, faith touches." What does this paragraph teach about Jesus?

_____

_____

5. *Power restricted (6:1-6a)*. Account for the unbelief of Jesus' countrymen (6:6a).

_____

_____

Why were they "offended at him" (6:3)?

_____

_____

Why does familiarity often breed contempt?

_____

_____

What is sad about this paragraph?

_____

_____

6. *Power delegated (6:6b-13)*. Why would Jesus give healing powers to His disciples?

_____

_____

Account for each of His instructions in verses 8-11.

_____

_____

7. *Power recognized (6:14-29)*. Note that most of this paragraph (vv. 17-29) is a parenthesis in Mark's account. The main point of the paragraph is given in verses 14-16. What is it?

_____

_____

Can you think of any reasons that Mark includes this comparatively long parenthesis in his story at this point? In answering this, think of Jesus' immediate future (cf. Luke 13:31-32) and also the setting of the disciples' recent "successes" and forthcoming trials.

_____

_____

_____

8. *Power at rest (6:30-32)*. What occupied the apostles' mind, as of verse 30?

_____

_____

What kind of a need did Jesus recognize, as of verse 31?

_____

_____

III. NOTES

1. *"Virtue had gone out of him" (5:30)*. The word "virtue" should read "power" as in 13:26.

2. *"Talitha cumi" (5:41)*. Mark retains the vernacular Aramaic words of Jesus to bring out the intimacy of His tone as He spoke to the young damsel in the language of the inner home circle.

3. *"His own country" (6:1)*. This was Nazareth and its environs.

4. *"Carpenter" (6:3)*. This is the only reference in the Bible that reveals Jesus' occupation before embarking on His public ministry.

5. *"Brother of James" (6:3)*. The brothers and sisters mentioned in this verse were born some time after Jesus. James and Jude are the authors of New Testament epistles.

6. *"Scrip" (6:8)*. This was a traveling bag for carrying provisions.

7. *"Shake off the dust . . . for a testimony against them" (6:11)*. Such an action was "not in personal animosity but as a testimony to show the seriousness of rejecting the message of the Son of God."[2]

8. *"King Herod" (6:14)*. This was Herod Antipas, son of Herod the Great and tetrarch of Galilee and Perea.

9. *"Apostles" (6:30)*. This is the only appearance of this word in Mark's gospel. The Greek word *apostolos* means "one sent forth." (Read 6:7 in this connection.)

IV. FOR THOUGHT AND DISCUSSION

1. What have you learned about Jesus' compassion from your study of this passage? Concerning the stories of Jairus's daughter and the woman with the blood disease, Morgan writes, "We have here a wonderful revelation of the understanding of Jesus. I think that is one of the most wonderful qualities in human love and friendship. Understandingness!"[3]

2. How is faith related to fear? Can sorrow and trial generate faith in the heart of a person? Do you think Christ can calm a storm in the heart of a person today? Has He ever done it in your heart? What are the conditions for such a miracle?

3. "I believe in miracles, for I believe in God." How do the stories of this lesson illustrate this line from one of our Christian songs?

4. How are work and rest related in Christian service? Does a Christian worker err in "working himself to death"? What is the purpose of rest?

2. C.F. Peiffer and E.F. Harrison, eds., *The Wycliffe Bible Commentary*, p. 1000.
3. G. Campbell Morgan, *The Gospel According to Mark*, p. 129.

V. FURTHER STUDY

Two subjects suggested for further study are:
1. What the Bible teaches about miracles[4]
2. A comparative study of the titles "apostle" and "disciple" in the New Testament

VI. WORDS TO PONDER

And he was ... asleep on a pillow: and they awake him ... (4:38).

"The rush of the storm, and the sweep of the wind did not wake Him; but the touch of the trembling hand, and the cry of men in trouble, did."[5]

---

4. A recommended commentary on Jesus' miracles is Richard C. Trench, *Notes on the Miracles of Our Lord* (London: Society for Promoting Christian Knowledge, 1904). For an apologetic defense of miracles, see C.S. Lewis, *Miracles* (New York: Macmillan, 1947).
5. Morgan, p. 102.

Renewed Surge of Opposition

In the passage of this lesson, Mark continues to report highlights of Jesus' ministry in Galilee. Miracles abound in the story, but Mark also reports the renewed surge of opposition to Jesus by religious leaders from Jerusalem. Read 7:1-2, and observe on Chart B where this point in Mark's gospel is located in the life of Christ. Chart K will help you fix in your mind the time of 7:1.

CONTEXT OF MARK 6:33—8:26   **Chart K**

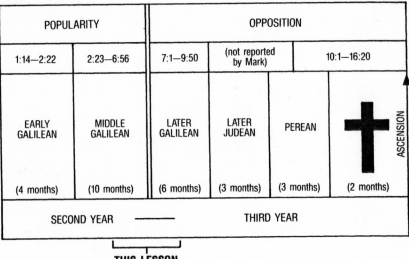

POPULARITY		OPPOSITION			
1:14—2:22	2:23—6:56	7:1—9:50	(not reported by Mark)		10:1—16:20
EARLY GALILEAN	MIDDLE GALILEAN	LATER GALILEAN	LATER JUDEAN	PEREAN	ASCENSION
(4 months)	(10 months)	(6 months)	(3 months)	(3 months)	(2 months)
SECOND YEAR ——— THIRD YEAR					

THIS LESSON

Observe from this chart that this lesson covers the last of the middle Galilean period and the first of the later Galilean period.

I. PREPARATION FOR STUDY

1. John's gospel reports more than does Mark's about the collapse of Jesus' Galilean campaign. Read John 6:22-71 and observe why the Jews rejected Jesus as their Messiah at this time. Note also that some of His disciples forsook Him about the same time (John 6:60-67).

2. Study the following geographical outline of Jesus' Galilean campaigns. Locate the various places on the map, and relate the outline to Chart B. Keep this setting in mind as you study the passage of this lesson (6:33–8:26).

Middle Galilean Period (the last ten months of the second year)
   1. To Jerusalem and return—Mark 2:23–3:6
   2. Near the Sea of Galilee—3:7-19*a*
   3. Throughout Galilee—3:19*b*-30 (prominence of Word ministry)
   4. By the sea—4:1–5:43 (prominence of Works ministry)
   5. Throughout Galilee—6:1-32
   6. By the sea—6:33-56

> STRONG OPPOSITION SETS IN   (cf. John 6:22-71)

Later Galilean Period (the first six months of the third year)
   1. To the northwest (Tyre and Sidon)—Mark 7:1-30
   2. To the southeast (Decapolis)—Mark 7:31–8:9
   3. To the northeast (from Dalmanutha to Caesarea Philippi) —Mark 8:10–9:29
   4. Secret return to Capernaum—Mark 9:30-50

II. ANALYSIS

Segments to be analyzed: 6:33-56 and 7:1–8:26
Paragraph divisions: at verses 6:33, 45; 7:1, 14, 24, 31; 8:1, 11, 22

A. Segment 6:33-56

Read this passage carefully, and record what is taught about each of these subjects:
1. The disciples' needs:

_____

_____

_____

2. Jesus' training of the twelve:

_____

_____

_____

3. The multitude's needs:

_____

_____

_____

4. Jesus' ministry to the multitudes:

_____

_____

_____

B. Segment 7:1–8:26

1. Compare the opening statement of 7:1 with that of 6:30. This is Mark's way of reporting how the enemies were beginning to close in on Jesus.
2. Read the entire passage, and record the main point of each paragraph.
7:1

_____

7:14

_____

7:24

_____

7:31

_____

8:1

_____

8:11

_____

8:22

_____

3. Which paragraphs are about the opposition?

_____

_____

What charges are made against Jesus and His disciples?

_____

List the many truths taught by Jesus in His replies to the opposition.

_____

4. What paragraphs report more miracles of Jesus?

_____

What do they contribute in answering the question as to who Jesus is?

_____

_____

III. NOTES

1. *"Brake the loaves, and gave them to his disciples" (6:41).* The tense of the Greek verb for "gave" calls for this translation: "kept giving." Thus the miracle of multiplication took place in Jesus' hands, between the breaking and the distributing.

2. *"Tradition of the elders" (7:3).* In Jesus' day the oral and written traditions of the Jews far outnumbered the laws of Scripture. Morgan writes this of tradition: "The law of God must be kept separate and apart . . . from any human interpretation of it, which is a tradition."[1] Also, "the first movement toward the mastery of the soul by tradition is the movement of that soul away from immediate, direct, first-hand fellowship with God."[2]

3. *"It is Corban [gift]" (7:1).* The *New Bible Commentary* explains this hypocritical device:

1. G. Campbell Morgan, *The Gospel According to Mark*, p. 158.
2. Ibid., p. 161.

The law concerning duty to parents was plain, but the Jews, with characteristic sophistry, had devised a means of evading it, even under the cloak of piety. A son could pledge his money to be paid into the temple treasury. This could be done in an ideal sense without any actual payment being made, or the payment could be deferred until after his death. He could even do it in a fit of anger, and could then tell his old parents in their time of need that he could offer them no help, since his money was Corban, i.e., dedicated under oath.[3]

4. *"Children" (7:27).* In Jesus' illustration the "children" represented the Jews. The "dogs" (more accurately, "little dogs," which were the household pets) represented the Gentiles. By this illustration Jesus was telling the Gentile woman that His mission was first to the Jews, who then were responsible to share the gospel with the whole world. In fact, His appearance in the Gentile territory of Tyre and Sidon[4] was not to minister to the multitudes there but to avoid those seeking Him in Galilee (7:24).

5. *"Leaven of the Pharisees" (8:15).* The leaven, or sin, of the Pharisees was hypocrisy (cf. Luke 12:1). Henry Alford says the "leaven of Herod" refers to "the irreligious lives and fawning worldly practices of the hangers-on of the court of Herod."[5]

IV. FOR THOUGHT AND DISCUSSION

Among the many applications that may be made from this passage, consider the following:

1. What Christians serving Christ today need to learn and practice
2. How tradition and formalism can deaden the work of the church
3. Why the heart of man must be right with God
4. The need of compassion on the part of Christians today

Below are some key statements in the passage of this lesson. If you are studying in a group, let the members share with each other what they have learned from these.

"They were as sheep not having a shepherd" (6:34).
"Give *ye* them to eat" (6:37).
"He departed into a mountain to pray" (6:46).
"Be of good cheer: it is I" (6:50).

3. F. Davidson et al., *The New Bible Commentary*, p., 820.
4. This is the only time in the record of the four gospels when Jesus goes to Gentile cities outside of Palestine.
5. Henry Alford, *The Greek Testament*, rev. ed. (Chicago: Moody, 1958), 1: 365.

"In vain do they worship me" (7:7).
"Making the word of God of none effect" (7:13).
"He hath done all things well" (7:37).
"How is it that ye do not understand?" (8:21).

V. FURTHER STUDY

1. Study Jesus' various *methods* of working miracles, as shown in this passage. Compare these with the methods of earlier miracles. Account for the varieties.

2. Study further into the reason for Christ's limiting His preaching tours to Jewish cities and villages. Consider such passages as Matthew 10:6 and 15:24.

VI. WORDS TO PONDER

This people honoureth me with their lips, but their heart is far from me. (Mark 7:6, quoting Isa. 29:13).

Lesson 9

The Turning Point of Jesus' Public Ministry

This is the crisis point of Jesus' public ministry, where He turned toward His death and resurrection. As Jesus reminisced with His disciples about the two-and-one-half years of ministering to the multitudes that He had just completed, His one great concern was, "Who do the people say I am?" According to the disciples' answer (8:28), He had failed to get across to the people who He really was. It must have been gratifying to hear Peter's reply, "Thou art the Christ," when Jesus directed the question to Peter personally.

We know that this conversation between Jesus and the twelve marked a turning point in Jesus' ministry, because now for the first time He began to tell His disciples explicitly that He must die and be raised again the third day (8:31). He had hinted at this before, and had foretold the events in parables and figures (e.g., John 2:19; 3:14), but He had not spelled it all out openly (cf. 8:23*a*).

Jesus was miles away from Jerusalem at the pivotal point of 8:27-30. On His way to the holy city His attention would be focused on His disciples, to prepare them for the months and years ahead. He would also have limited contacts with the multitudes and intense discussions with His opponents. These are the general subjects of the next few chapters of Mark, which we shall be studying.

I. PREPARATION FOR STUDY

1. As a review, complete this key outline of Mark without looking at the survey Chart D.

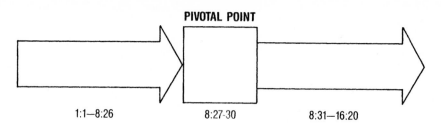

PIVOTAL POINT

| 1:1—8:26 | 8:27-30 | 8:31—16:20 |

2. Think back over 1:1–8:26, and recall different identifications that Jesus made of Himself, directly or indirectly. List these.

_____

_____

_____

3. Locate Caesarea Philippi (8:27) on the map. As you study the remainder of Mark's gospel, keep in mind this *general* itinerary of Jesus for 8:31–16:20.

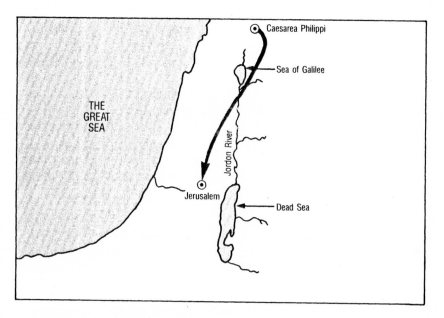

4. Study the context of the passage of this lesson (8:27–9:50) on survey Chart D. Note especially the outline on page 64.

71

8:31	11:1	14:1	16:1
Jesus as Redeemer	Jesus as Lord	Jesus as Sacrifice	Jesus as the Living One

5. You will note that the passage of this lesson is divided into three segments. You would do well to study the lesson in at least three different units in order to devote sufficient time to each segment.

II. ANALYSIS

Segments to be analyzed: 8:27–9:1; 9:2-32; and 9:33-50
Paragraph divisions: at verses 8:27, 31, 34; 9:2, 9, 14, 30, 33, 38, 43 (mark these in your Bible)

The unfinished analytical Chart L should be used to record your observations as you study 8:27–9:1. Look for items beyond those suggested in the study questions given below. Make outlines similar to the one shown.

A. General Analysis: Segment 8:27–9:1

Who is the main speaker of this segment?

_____

_____

Observe how many key truths of Christ's redemptive ministry are recorded in this short passage. Compare this with the many long passages earlier in the gospel devoted to such things as miracles.

B. Paragraph Analysis: Segment 8:27–9:1

1. *Person of Christ (8:27-30).* What do you think is the key statement of the paragraph?

_____

_____

Account for the words "revelation" and "vindication" on Chart L.

_____

_____

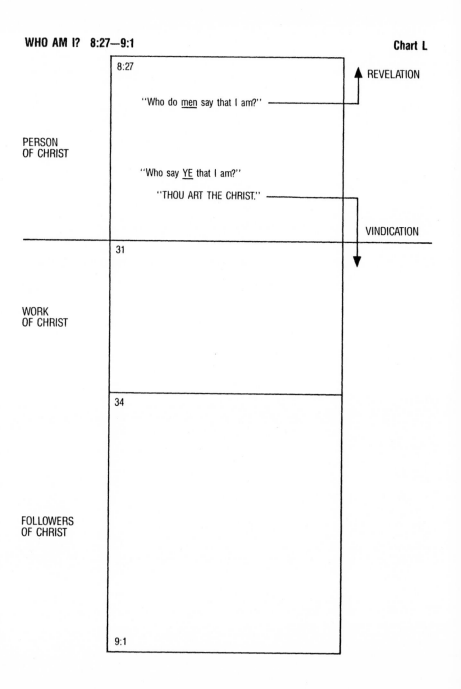

REVELATION

8:27

"Who do <u>men</u> say that I am?"

PERSON
OF CHRIST

"Who say <u>YE</u> that I am?"

"THOU ART THE CHRIST."

VINDICATION

31

WORK
OF CHRIST

34

FOLLOWERS
OF CHRIST

9:1

73

2. *Work of Christ (8:31-33).* What is suggested by the word "began" in verse 31?

_____

_____

In the Greek text the word "must" appears immediately after the word "that." What is Mark thereby emphasizing?

_____

_____

Relate this word "must" to the phrase "things . . . of God" (8:33). Compare also Acts 4:28.

_____

_____

Explain Jesus' command "Get thee behind me, Satan" (8:33).

_____

_____

3. *Followers of Christ (8:34—9:1).* Be sure to record the key words and phrases of this paragraph in the box of Chart L. What are the different parts of the invitation of 8:34?

_____

_____

What is the strength of the word "will" (8:34)? Why is this word a key to a person's salvation?

_____

_____

Explain "take up his cross."

_____

_____

How do verses 35-38 interpret and illustrate the invitation of verse 34?

_____

_____

Compare the words "cross" (8:34) and "power' (9:1).

_____

_____

C. General Analysis: Segments 9:2-32 and 9:33-50

Analyze in detail these two segments separately. Before doing that, however, read the entire passage, and observe the various ways Jesus was training His disciples. This is the main subject of this passage. Spend much time here, recording your studies below.

Jesus' Training of the Twelve (9:2-50)
9:2-8:

_____

_____

9:9-13:

_____

_____

9:14-29:

_____

_____

9:30-32:

_____

_____

9:33-37:

_____

_____

9:38-42:

_____

_____

9:43-50:

_____

_____

_____

D. Paragraph Analysis: Segments 9:2-32 and 9:33-50

1. *Paragraph 9:2-8.* May this transfiguration have been what Jesus foretold in 9:1? (See *Notes.*)

_____

_____

What did Moses personify in Old Testament history?

_____

Elias?

_____

_____

What was wrong about Peter's request?

_____

How do verses 7 and 8 show Jesus as the preeminent One?

_____

Why did God give this mountaintop experience to the disciples?

_____

2. *Paragraph 9:9-13.* What two subjects were the disciples questioning? (vv. 10-11)?

_____

The question about Elias (Elijah) arose over the transfiguration experience. For the prophecy about Elijah, read Malachi 4:5-6. For an interpretation of "Elias is indeed come," read Matthew 11:13-14; 17:13. Also read Mark 9:11-13 in a modern paraphrase, such as *The Living Bible*, for help in understanding the flow of this conversation.

3. *Paragraph 9:14-29.* Study the subject of faith in this paragraph, in the light of these statements:

"O faithless generation, how long shall I be with you?" (9:19).

"If thou canst believe, all things are possible to him that believeth" (9:23).

"Lord, I believe; help thou mine unbelief" (9:24). (Is this statement a contradiction?)

"This kind can come forth by nothing, but by prayer and fasting" (9:29).

4. *Paragraph 9:30-32.* Read the first phrase of verse 31 as "For he kept on teaching." How is fear ("were afraid") related to ignorance ("understood not") (9:32)?

_____

_____

5. *Paragraph 9:33-37.* What recent event may have brought on the dispute reported here?

_____

_____

What was Jesus' method of correcting His disciples?

_____

_____

6. *Paragraph 9:38-42.* What important truths is Jesus teaching here?

_____

_____

7. *Paragraph 9:43-50.* What are the key repeated words and phrases of this paragraph?

_____

_____

On verses 44, 46, 48, read the last verse of Isaiah (66:24). What are the spiritual lessons taught by "salt" in 9:49-50? (Cf. Matt. 5:13.)

_____

_____

Compare "peace" of 9:50 with the dispute of 9:34.

_____

_____

III. NOTES

1. *"Whosoever shall lose his life . . . shall save it" (8:35).* "This is not a description of the way of salvation for the lost, but rather of the philosophy of life for the disciple."[1] (Cf. Phil. 1:21). The same principle is involved in both, however.

2. *"The kingdom of God come with power" (9:1).* Three interpretations of this prophecy of Jesus that have been suggested are: (1) the transfiguration of 9:2ff.; (2) the resurrection and ascension; (3) Pentecost and the missionary outreach of the book of Acts.

3. *"Transfigured" (9:2).* The compound Greek word used here suggests a change of the essential form of Jesus, rather than mere outward appearance. Vincent writes, "There was a fact and a

1. C.f. Pfeiffer and E.F. Harrison, eds., *The Wycliffe Bible Commentary*, p. 1006.

power in that vision which mere radiance and the appearance of the dead patriarchs could not wholly convey: a revelation of Deity breaking out in that glorified face and form, which appealed to something deeper than sense, and confirmed the words from heaven: *This is my beloved Son.*"[2] The "high mountain" where the transfiguration took place was probably Mount Hermon (9,200 feet), about twelve miles northeast of Caesarea Philippi.

4. *"Little ones" (9:42).* This may be a literal reference to children or to believers immature and underdeveloped in faith.[3]

5. *"Their worm dieth not" (9:44).* The picture is associated with the refuse heap located in the valley of Hinnom (*Gehenna*, which is the Greek word translated "hell" in this context). (Cf. 2 Kings 23:10.)

IV. FOR THOUGHT AND DISCUSSION

1. What must be the Christian's constant attitude of heart regarding Satan? (Cf. Mark 8:33 and James 4:7.)

2. What does it mean for a believer to "take up his cross" (8:34)?

3. In what ways can you nurture a spirit of "Christ above all" in your life?

4. Why is humility an important virtue in Christian service?

5. Can you think of examples of exclusivism and sectarianism in the work of the church today? What can Christians do to correct such evils?

6. Are there various *degrees* of believing? Do doubts in one's heart cancel out all faith?

7. Which is easier for a Christian: to have a mountaintop experience (such as 9:2-8) or to minister in the valley (such as 9:14-29)? In what ways is Christ sufficient for both experiences?

V. FURTHER STUDY

Although the two words "and fasting" (9:29) do not appear in some of the best Greek manuscripts, the evidence for their exclusion is inconclusive. With the aid of a concordance and other sources, make a study of prayer and fasting in the New Testament.

VI. WORDS TO PONDER

I believe; help thou mine unbelief (9:24).
I do have faith, but not enough. Help me! (TEV).

---

2. Marvin R. Vincent, *Word Studies in the New Testament,* 1:100.
3. See *The Wycliffe Bible Commentary,* p. 1008.

Lesson 10

Mark 10:1-52

Concluding Ministries in Perea

Mark skips over the next five months of Jesus' public ministry, reporting only the last of His ministries. They were in Perea, the region on the east side of the Jordan (10:1). Read 10:1, and then refer to Chart B again and observe where chapter 10 appears in the chronological timetable of Jesus' career.

When we keep in mind that Jesus left Caesarea Philippi to go to Jerusalem to be crucified (Lesson 9) and that He never sought to postpone His death, then we will see that His ministries for the next six months in Judea and Perea (Chart B) were not delay tactics but foreordained appointments of a divine calendar. In short, Jesus went to Perea because it was not yet His time to die. He had a work to do in those regions in the meantime. Our study of this lesson is about that work.

JESUS' PUBLIC MINISTRY BEFORE PASSION WEEK　　　　　　**Chart M**

FIRST YEAR		—	SECOND YEAR		—	THIRD YEAR		
OBSCURITY			POPULARITY			OPPOSITION		
OPENING EVENTS	EARLY MINISTRIES		EXTENDED MINISTRIES			SPECIALIZED MINISTRY	CONCLUDING MINISTRIES	
4 months	8 months EARLY JUDEAN		4 months EARLY GALILEAN	10 months MIDDLE GALILEAN		6 months LATER GALILEAN	3 months LATER JUDEAN	3 months PEREAN

SEE CHART N

79

I. PREPARATION FOR STUDY

For more help in seeing what transpired in Jesus' career between Mark 9 and Mark 10,[1] study Charts M and N. As you will see, Chart M is a condensed version of Chart B, and Chart N is an amplification of one section of Chart M.

CONCLUDING MINISTRIES OF JESUS (an excerpt of Chart M)   **Chart N**

LATER JUDEAN PERIOD			PEREAN PERIOD		
Part One (1 week)	Part Two (2 months)	Part Three (1 week)	Part One	Interruption (brief interval)	Part Two
JERUSALEM (Feast of Tabernacles)	REGIONS OF JUDEA	JERUSALEM (Feast of Dedication)	REGIONS OF PEREA	BETHANY	REGIONS OF PEREA
JESUS AND JEWISH RULERS	EVANGELISM (special tour of 70 disciples)	JESUS AND JEWISH RULERS	EVANGELISM	MIRACLE (Lazarus)	EVANGELISM

THIS LESSON

II. ANALYSIS

Segment to be analyzed: 10:1-52
Paragraph divisions: at verses 1, 13, 17, 23, 28, 32, 35, 41, 46

A. General Analysis

A pattern in the order of events of Mark 10 is not clear. Before analyzing each paragraph separately, view the segment as a whole, and attempt to see connections between the paragraphs.
1. First, read each paragraph, and record paragraph titles on Chart O.
2. Study Chart O carefully. What six paragraphs are about the general subject of the kingdom?

_____

_____

1. Divine inspiration of selectivity is the basis for a Bible author's exclusion as well as inclusion of any parts of the total story. Luke and John are our main sources for this material left out of Mark (Luke 10:1–13:21; John 7:10–10:39).

Note that the other three paragraphs are set off from these on the chart, identified by the subjects "Opposition," "Prediction," and "Miracle." The location of each of the three paragraphs in the chapter is based on a geographical (not topical) reason. Read verses 1, 32, and 46 for the geographical references. Note on Chart O that the last paragraph is a transitional paragraph, for Jesus is here on His way from Perea to Jerusalem (read 11:1).[2]

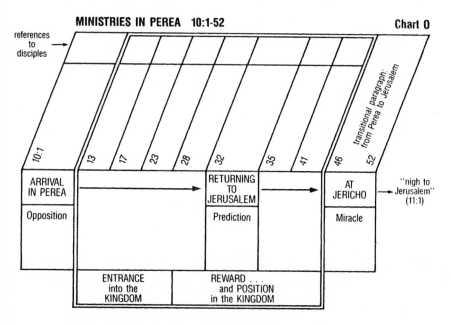

3. Read through the chapter again and note every reference to disciples of Jesus. Record these on Chart O. What does this reveal about one of the main purposes of Jesus' Perean ministry?

_____

_____

B. Paragraph Analysis

1. *Paragraph 10:1-12.* What was the Pharisees' tactic here?

_____

_____

2. Obviously Jericho (10:46-52) is not in Perea.

What does Jesus teach about marriage and divorce?

_____

Read Matthew 19:9 for the exception cited in that gospel.
2. *Paragraph 10:13-16.* Account for the disciples' action in verse 13.

_____

_____

Explain the statements:
"of such is the kingdom of God" (10:14)

_____

"receive the kingdom of God as a little child" (10:15)

_____

3. *Paragraph 10:17-22.* In your own words, what was the one hindrance to the rich man's salvation?

_____

_____

Compare the commands of verse 21: go, sell, give; come, take up, follow.

_____

Compare "treasure in heaven" (v. 21) and "great possessions" (v. 22).

_____

Explain Jesus' words of verse 18. Was He denying His deity?

_____

4. *Paragraph 10:23-27.* What brought on this discussion?

_____

_____

Compare the words "hard" (vv. 23-24) and "impossible" (v. 27).

_____

Why did Jesus use such an illustration as that of verse 25?

_____

In the light of Jesus' words, evaluate this statement: "It is impossible for a rich man to enter into the kingdom of God."

_____

What does verse 27 reveal about salvation?

_____

5. *Paragraph 10:28-31.* What brought on Peter's statement of verse 28?

_____

Compare these rewards:
    a hundredfold—now in this time
    eternal life—in the world to come
How does the phrase "with persecutions" qualify the rewards of verse 30?

_____

Explain verse 30 in the context of this paragraph.

_____

6. *Paragraph 10:32-34.* Analyze each phrase of verse 32. What impresses you about this reporting of Mark?

_____

_____

Why do you think Jesus kept repeating His prophecy of the near events (10:33-34)?

_____

7. *Paragraph 10:35-40.* What must have been in the hearts of James and John for them to make the presumptuous request of verse 37? (For one thing, recall 9:2.)

_____

In verse 38 Jesus relates the disciples' request to His cup and baptism. Why? (See *Notes* for the symbolism of the cup and baptism.)

_____

What did Jesus mean by His statement of verse 40?

_____

8. *Paragraph 10:41-45.* How does Jesus measure greatness?

_____

Note that these words about greatness are the context for the key verse of Mark (10:45). Recall from your earlier survey studies (e.g., Chart D) that the section 8:31–10:52 is called *Jesus as Redeemer*. This is because at 8:31 Jesus' main attention is diverted from the *serving* phase of His work to the *redemptive* phase (dying). Observe in 10:45 that Jesus' life is what is given as a ransom. And yet He is the one who is our Redeemer—that is, the one who *buys back* our souls. To whom is this ransom paid?

_____

Compare these two statements of Jesus:
v. 43: Whosoever will be *great* among you shall be your *minister* (the Greek word is *diakonos*, translated "servant," "deacon").
v. 44: Whosoever of you will be the *chiefest* shall be *servant* of all (the Greek word is *doulos*, translated "bondslave").

9. *Paragraph 10:46-52.* How was this miracle a vindication of Jesus' claim to messiahship? Answer this in light of Bartimeus's cry for help (vv. 47-48).

_____

_____

_____

III. NOTES

1. *"Bill of divorcement" (10:4).* The Mosaic regulation, with its condition overlooked by the Pharisees, is given in Deuteronomy 24:1.

2. *"Why callest thou me good" (10:18).* Jesus is not here correcting the young man but indirectly showing him that since He is absolutely good, He must be God. Of Jesus' sinlessness, Morgan writes, "If there is one thing more noticeable than another in the revelation of this Person in the four Gospels, it is His quiet, insistent, and unhesitating claim to sinlessness."[3] (Cf. John 8:46.)

3. *"Cup . . . baptism" (10:38).* From Mark 14:36 and Luke 12:50 we learn that these two symbols spoke of Jesus' coming suffering and death.

4. *"A ransom for [literally, in the place of] many" (10:45).* The word "ransom" was used often in Jesus' day when referring to the price paid to free a slave.

IV. FOR THOUGHT AND DISCUSSION

1. Why did God decree the marriage bond to be indissoluble? How do you account for the high percentage of divorces today?
2. What does Mark 10 teach about:
   a. the heart attitude necessary for salvation?
   b. the motives, works, and rewards of discipleship?
3. How can pride and selfishness in Christian service be conquered?

V. FURTHER STUDY

Inquire further into the New Testament teaching of (1) marriage and the home; (2) the deity of Christ; (3) the doctrine of redemption.

3. G. Campbell Morgan, *The Gospel According to Mark*, p. 232.

VI. WORDS TO PONDER

The Son of Man did not come to be served but to serve . . .

"Had the great statement ended at that point, we should have stood in awe in the presence of this Self-emptying of Jesus, but we should have heard no Gospel. In the final words of the declaration we hear the Gospel, and the music of the evangel breaks upon the soul."[4]

. . . and to give His life a ransom for many (10:45, *Berkeley*).

4. Ibid, p. 244.

Lesson 11

Jesus as Lord

J esus now arrives in Jerusalem and begins His activities for the first three days of Passion Week.[1] All four gospels begin to report this last week of Jesus' public ministry comparatively early in their text.[2] This is because of the week's importance. That was the week for which Jesus was born. Everything else He did and said led up to this and found its meaning in it. The cross was the crucial experience for Christ, because death and Satan were conquered in it. Jesus' crown was made possible by the cross.

Jesus' visits to the Temple during Passion Week were the occasion for open hostility against Him by His enemies, through verbal attacks at public gatherings. Basically, their charge was "By what authority are You doing these things?" (11:28, *Berkeley*). In this they were challenging His claim to lordship. But Jesus' clear and strong answers killed every charge. This is all part of the sad story of Jesus' kinsmen the Jews' rejecting Him, bringing on the hour when He finally had to reject them (12:9). Our study of this passage will reveal a portrait of *Jesus as Lord* in confrontation with the rulers of darkness. (Observe the context of the title "Lord of lords and King of kings" in Rev. 17:14 and 19:16, where Jesus confronts His enemies.)

I. PREPARATION FOR STUDY

1. Study Chart P to become acquainted with the general ministry of Jesus during Passion Week. Also observe on the chart where each day begins in the account of Mark. Read John 11:55–12:1, from which we learn that Passion Week led up to the great Pass-

1. The week of Jesus' life climaxing in His death is usually called Passion Week.
2. The biblical record of Passion Week, up to the crucifixion, takes up about one-third of both Matthew and John, one-fourth of Mark, and one-seventh of Luke.

over holiday of the Jews. Why do you think it was in the divine plan for Jesus to be in the vicinity of Jerusalem during this season?

_____

_____

PASSION WEEK   MARK 11:1—15:46
KING EXTOLLED
RIDING
INTO THE CITY
ON A COLT
(Mark 11:1-10)

Chart P
KING MOCKED
DRIVEN OUT
OF THE CITY
BEARING A CROSS
(John 19:17; cf. Mark 15:20-21)

11:1	11:12	11:20 14:11	no Bible record	14:12	14:26 15:46
SUN.	MON.	TUES.	WED.	THURS.	FRI.
MINISTRY TO PUBLIC (cf. Luke 21:37-38)			MINISTRY TO DISCIPLES		SOLITARY MINISTRY
ACTIVE DAYS			QUIET DAYS		VIOLENT DAY
authority			compassion		submission
Jesus speaks much					Jesus speaks little

2. Review the opposition to Jesus as recorded in Mark thus far. Who have been the main opponents and what were some of their charges?

_____

_____

Have the multitudes turned against Jesus yet?

_____

_____

3. Plan to study this lesson in at least three different units—for example, one unit per segment. This is recommended because of the length of the passage involved.

II. ANALYSIS

Segments to be analyzed: 11:1-14;[3] 11:15–12:44; 13:1-37
Paragraph divisions: at verses 11:1, 11, 12, 15, 20, 27; 12:1, 13, 18, 28, 35, 38, 41; 13:1, 9, 14, 21, 24, 28, 32

A. General Anslysis: Mark's Record of the First Three Days of Passion Week

Before you study each of the three segments separately, read the three chapters (11:1–13:37) first, for an overall view of the action. Chart Q is a survey chart of this passage. Study the various outlines shown, and use the chart to record further observations.
1. Note the threefold outline at the top of the chart. This is how the passage of this lesson is divided into three segments. On the basis of your reading of 11:1–13:37, which segment records action mostly: _____; discourse mostly: _____; interrogation mostly: _____?
2. Record your paragraph titles on the chart.
3. What paragraphs are about opposition to Jesus?

_____

_____

Record the various charges made and who the opponents are. Where did most of the confrontation with Jesus take place? (See the geography outline.)

_____

_____

Observe on the chart that Mark does not record any opposition in the opening paragraph of each new day.
4. What paragraphs make reference to the disciples?

_____

_____

3. There are various possibilities as to how the passage 11:1–12:44 could be divided into different segments. In this manual 11:1-14 is separated from 11:15–12:44 because in it Mark chooses not to write about the opposition yet (cf. Luke 19:39-44; Matt. 21:15-17), but to mention only Jesus' relationship to His disciples and the multitudes.

For whose immediate benefit did Jesus give the discourse of chapter 13?

_____

_____

5. Record on Chart Q in brief outline the various teachings of Jesus reported in the different paragraphs.
6. What are your general impressions of the first three days of Passion Week, after making this overall study?

_____

_____

_____

B. Segment Analysis

1. *First appearance in Jerusalem (11:1-14)*
March into Jerusalem (11:1-10). What prophecies did Jesus make, and when were they fulfilled?

_____

_____

What lessons was Jesus teaching His disciples through this?

_____

Read Zechariah 9:9 for the Old Testament prophecy of this event. Read Psalm 118:25-26, keeping in mind that "Hosanna" of Mark 11:9 represents the Hebrew meaning literally "Save, we pray!" By the time of Jesus the word was used more as praise to the Saviour than prayer for salvation. Psalm 118 was one of the Hallel psalms (113–118) recited often at the Passover festival.[4] In view of this, what do you think the multitudes were acclaiming Jesus to be at this time?

_____

_____

---

4. Jesus quotes from Psalm 118 a little later in Mark (12:10-11).

FIRST THREE DAYS OF PASSION WEEK 11:1—13:37

Chart Q

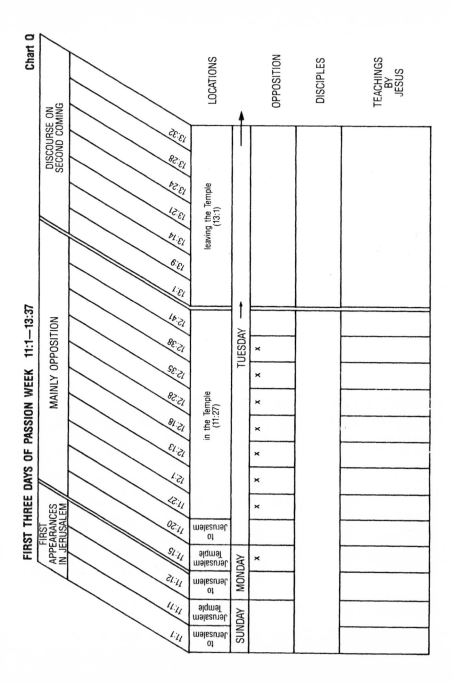

What were they expecting Him to do once He arrived at the Temple, in the heart of the holy city?

_____

_____

How did they interpret the messianic kingdom (11:9-10; cf. John 6:22-59)?

_____

Compare the cry of "Hosanna!" at this time and the frenzied demand "Crucify him!" five days later (15:13).

_____

What do you think the disciples were thinking as they marched with Jesus into the city?

_____

Do you think they were among those who "went before"or those who "followed" (11:9)?

_____

Why is this march of Jesus called His "triumphal entry"?

_____

First view of the Temple (11:11). Mark sums up Jesus' first visit to the Temple in just a few words. What does He suggest by these phrases?
"when he had looked round about upon all things"[5]

_____

_____

5. G. Campbell Morgan calls this "the look of investigation, the look of inquisition, the look of One Who had the right so to look, the look of the supreme and final authority; it was also the look of the heart of an infinite compassion, the look of the eyes bedewed with tears"(*The Gospel According to Mark*, p. 256).

"with the twelve"

Fig tree cursed (11:12-14). The sequel to this event did not take place until the next day (11:20-26). The main point is to be found in Jesus' decree of verse 14. Mark makes a special point of reporting that Jesus' disciples heard that decree. If you were one of the disciples, what might have been your thoughts at this time? (See *Notes* concerning the time of a fig tree's fruit. Also, read Hos. 9:10; Luke 13:6-9.)

---

2. *Jesus answers His opponents (11:15–12:44).*
For each paragraph of this segment identify the following: (1) the occasion of or reason for the opposition; (2) who the opponents are; (3) Jesus' defense and related teachings.
Temple cleansing (11:15-19). Is there anything miraculous about the actions of verses 15 and 16?

Read Isaiah 56:7 for Jesus' quote of Mark 11:17. In view of Isaiah 56:1*a* and the phrase "my house" of Mark 11:17, who does Jesus here claim to be?

What were the two different effects of this Temple cleansing (v. 18)?

Instructions to the disciples on prayer (11:20-26). According to both Matthew and Mark, the question of the disciples concerning the fig tree is not the *why* of Jesus' curse but the *how* of the withering (see Matt. 21:20). If Jesus had intended a spiritual lesson about hypocrisy on the previous day when He cursed the fig tree, He does not pursue this application now. What is the application here?

What condition is necessary for the answer to a prayer requesting a miracle?

_____

_____

What condition is necessary for the answer of a Christian's plea to God for forgiveness?

_____

_____

Source of authority (11:27-33). What does the phrase "these things" (11:28) refer to?

_____

_____

What was Jesus' strategy in answering this charge?

_____

_____

Would you say that *in effect* He did answer His opponents' question?

_____

_____

Parable of husbandmen (12:1-12). To whom did Jesus speak these words (cf. "them" of 12:1 with "they" and "the people" of 12:12)?

_____

_____

In what ways does Jesus identify Himself by the parable and by the prophecy of Psalm 118:22-23? (Read this prophecy.)

_____

_____

If the "husbandmen" represent the Jewish religious leaders plotting against Jesus, when was the prophecy of their destruction (v. 9) fulfilled in history?

_____

_____

Question of tribute (12:13-17). What is the strategy of the opposition here?

_____

_____

What does Jesus reveal about Himself by His reply?

_____

_____

Question of resurrection (12:18-27). Read Acts 23:8 for a reference to the Sadducees' doctrine. What are Jesus' two accusations of verse 24?

_____

_____

How does He support those accusations in verses 25-27?

_____

_____

The first commandment (12:28-34). What important teachings appear in this paragraph?

Explain Jesus' statement of verse 34.

_____

_____

Christ as Lord (12:35-37). Observe that Jesus brings the Old Testament again into His argument. (Read Ps. 110:1.) How had He done this in the two previous paragraphs?

_____

_____

Note the last sentence of this paragraph. Are the crowds still on Jesus side?

_____

_____

Hypocrisy (12:38-40). Can you think of any modern parallels to the hypocritical ways of the scribes mentioned here?

_____

_____

Unqualified devotion (12:41-44). This paragraph stands in bold contrast to the ones preceding it in the segment. Why must it have been a very heartening experience for Jesus to observe the poor widow's devotion, at this moment in His ministry?

_____

_____

Concerning the timing of this, A. T. Robertson writes:

> This is the last appearance of Jesus in the Temple. His public teaching is over save the words of defense in his trial and the seven sayings on the Cross. The Pharisees and Sadducees had withdrawn in terror at the explosion of the wrath of Jesus, and even the disciples were at some distance as Jesus sat alone by the treasury.[6]

Observe that Mark says that Jesus "called unto him his disciples" to show them what the poor widow was doing.

3. *Discourse on Jesus' second coming (13:1-37).*
A full study of this prophecy of Jesus (called the Olivet discourse because it was spoken while Jesus sat on the Mount of Olives— Mark 13:3) would include an analysis of the parallel in Matthew and Luke. (See *Further Study*.) Our present study will concentrate only on Mark's account. First read the chapter to get a feel of the discourse in general. Then consider the following important aspects of this prophecy, as it is related to the total prophetical content of Scripture.

   a. Prophecies of the Bible often have a double perspective. This is clearly true of the Olivet apocalypse. Jesus is prophesying about the coming destruction of Jerusalem (which took place in A.D. 70) as well as His second coming (yet future).

   b. Points and periods of time are not always easily identified in a passage of prophetic latitude, when long spaces like millenniums are involved. For example, phrases like "after those days" and "until" might represent an interim of a thousand years (e.g., Lukk. 21:24). Prophetical perspective is selective, describing not the full course of the ages but the key crises of that unwritten history.

   c. Any one prophecy in a Bible passage may omit an item recorded in a parallel prophecy. (E.g., only Luke reports explicitly the fall of Jerusalem and the Gentile period that followed, Luke 21:24.)

6. A. T. Robertson, *A Harmony of the Gospels for Students of the Life of Christ* (Nashville: Broadman, 1922), p. 172.

Chart R is a work sheet for recording your observations of the text of chapter 13. Observe the breakdown of paragraphs and the overall general outline. As you study each paragraph, record in the appropriate box what it contributes to the account. This will help you immeasurably in your analysis of Mark 13.

THE OLIVET DISCOURSE   MARK 13:1-37   Chart R

PARAGRAPHS	FALL OF JERUSALEM	—END OF THE AGE —SECOND COMING OF CHRIST	EXHORTATIONS	
13:1-8	vv. 1-4, Questions vv. 5-8, Opening Statements			INTRODUCTION
9-13				
14-20				DESCRIPTION
(LUKE 21:24—FIRST FALL OF JERUSALEM, FOLLOWED BY "TIMES OF THE GENTILES")				
21-23				
24-27		"Then shall they see the Son of man coming" (13:26).		
28-31				EXHORTATION
32-37				

The disciples' questions (13:1-4). Observe the sequence of (1) exclamation (v. 1); (2) prophecy (v. 2); (3) questions (v. 4). What two questions does Mark report? (Cf. Matt. 24:3)

_____

_____

From the Matthew passage we may conclude that the disciples viewed the destruction of the Temple, Christ's second coming,

and the end of the age as happening at the same time.[7] Whatever
their thoughts, Jesus' answer distinguished between the destruction of Jerusalem of A.D. 70 (cf. Mark 13:14; Luke 21:20-24) and His
coming at the end of the age (e.g., Mark 13:26). As you study this
Olivet discourse keep in mind the sequence of events shown on
Chart S.

OLIVET DISCOURSE **Chart S**

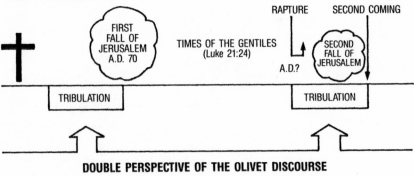

DOUBLE PERSPECTIVE OF THE OLIVET DISCOURSE

Opening statements (13:5-8). How could these opening words of
Jesus be viewed as introductory to the two prophecies of the fall
of Jerusalem and His second coming?

Observe the key warning, "Take heed" (v. 5), which appears
throughout the discourse.
Pretribulation signs (13:9-13). What different things did Jesus
prophesy here?

How soon did the persecutions of verse 9 come to the Christian
church? (Cf. Acts 4:5ff.; 5:27ff.; 12:1ff.; 24:1ff.; 25:1ff.)

Days of tribulation (13:14-20). Read Luke 21:20-24 for its specific
references to the not-distant fall of Jerusalem. Also read Daniel

7. The other view is that Matt. 24:3 suggests that the disciples saw the three
   events as being widely separated in time.

12:11[8] for the prophecy referred to in Mark 13:14. Daniel's prophecy reaches forward to the end of the Great Tribulation in the end times.[9] In what ways is Mark 13:14-20 a double prophecy?

Further exhortations (13:21-22). What are Jesus' warnings and exhortations at this point?

If the phrase "And then" (v. 21) intends to advance the chronological sequence of events, where would this paragraph be located timewise?

Posttribulation signs (13:24-27). What signs after the Tribulation will herald the coming of Christ?

Who are "the elect" of 13:27?

Why do you think Jesus concluded His prophecies with His reference to this _gathering_ of verse 27?

Exhortations based on what is known (13:28-31). Observe the repeated word "know." What is Jesus' appeal here?

Who is meant by "this generation" (v. 30)?

8. Cf. Dan. 9:27; 11:31.
9. The phrase "neither shall be" (v. 19) identifies this prophecy with this great tribulation, which shall be the worst of all tribulation times.

Why did Jesus make the statement of verse 31?

_____

_____

Exhortations based on what is not known (13:32-37). What are the key words and phrases of this paragraph?

_____

Explain the words "neither the Son" in verse 32.

_____

How is verse 37 an appropriate conclusion to Jesus' discourse?

_____

How does the verse relate to both prophecies of the fall of Jerusalem and the end times?

_____

_____

III. NOTES

1. *"The time of figs was not yet" (11:13).* At this early spring-time a normal fig tree bore early-ripe or "green" figs before the leaves appeared. After that came the "time of figs" (11:13). The fig tree that Jesus saw had "nothing but leaves," that is, there was no early-ripe figs, when there should have been. This may be seen as an illustration of hypocrisy, or pretension.

2. *"Money changers . . . doves" (11:15).* This Temple business was sponsored by the high priestly family. "The animals were sold for sacrificial purposes, and the money-changers exchanged the common currency for the half-shekel necessary to pay the temple tax."[10]

3. *"Farthing" (12:42).* This Roman coin was the equivalent of a fourth of a cent.

4. *"What manner of stones and what buildings" (13:1).* The Temple of Herod was impressive both as to beauty and size. A rabbinical saying was "He who has not seen the temple of Herod has

10. C.F. Pfeiffer and E.F. Harrison, eds., *The Wycliffe Bible Commentary*, p. 1012.

never seen a beautiful building." Some of the green and white marble stones were more than sixty feet long, seven feet high, and eight feet deep.

5. *"Abomination of desolation" (13:14).* The Temple was desecrated in various ways in the siege of Titus (A.D. 70). This was a foreshadow of the profaning of the Temple by Antichrist during the Great Tribulation (cf. 2 Thess. 2:3-4; Rev. 13:14-18).

6. *"Knoweth no man . . . neither the Son" (13:32).* This self-limitation by the Son is an illustration of the emptying described in Philippians 2:5-8. During Jesus' earthly career He exercised His divine attributes always at the Father's bidding (John 8:26-29). The fact of His divine-human nature is not negated by our inability to fully understand it.

IV. FOR THOUGHT AND DISCUSSION

1. Observe how Jesus usually moved from defense to offense when He answered the charges of His opponents. Why is a positive, forthright proclamation of the gospel so vital when the church is attacked by unbelievers?

2. Think more about faith in God and forgiveness of other people as being keys to successful praying.

3. Do you see hyprocrisy in Christian circles today? Is it possible that you are guilty of pretension in some area of your life? What is the cure for hypocrisy?

4. What should be the relationship of a Christian to his government? Answer this in the light of Mark 12:14-17 and Romans 13:1-7.

5. Make a list of at least ten important spiritual lessons taught by the Olivet Discourse.

V. FURTHER STUDY

1. Study Luke 19:37-44 for the further light on Jesus' triumphal entry into Jerusalem. Observe among other things the repeated word "peace."

2. Make a full comparative study of Matthew 24–25, Mark 13, and Luke 21 as they report the Olivet Discourse. Commentaries and books on prophecy will be of much help here.

3. How do you reconcile the unexpectedness of Christ's second coming ("ye know not when the master . . . cometh," 13:35) with

the prewarning of signs (13:29)? (Keep in mind the difference between the second coming and the rapture—Chart S.)

_____

_____

Why has God hidden from man the day and hour of Christ's return?

_____

_____

VI. WORDS TO PONDER

Take ye heed, watch and pray (13:33).

Events Prior to Jesus' Arrest

Nothing is reported in any of the four gospels concerning Wednesday of Passion Week. Apparently it was a quiet day for Jesus and His disciples, spent in rest and conference. For Jesus' enemies it was no doubt an active day of plotting how to do away with this Nazarene who claimed to be the Messiah. Actually, plotting such as this is the note on which Mark resumes his story of Jesus' last days on earth (14:1).

The passage of this lesson is about the moving drama leading up to the arrest of Jesus in the Garden of Gethsemane. As you study the text you will sense the pathos of it all and realize more than ever before that Jesus was truly a man, tried in all points "like as we are, yet without sin" (Heb. 4:15).

I. PREPARATION FOR STUDY

Acquaint yourself with the Jews' annual feast of Passover, which was the setting of 14:1-42.[1] (See *Notes.*) Among the Bible passages to read are Exodus 12; 23:17; Leviticus 23:4-8; Numbers 9:1-14; Deuteronomy 16:16. Consult a Bible dictionary for a description of the feast. For Paul's interpretation of Christ as our Passover, read 1 Corinthians 5:7-8.

II. ANALYSIS

Segment to be analyzed: 14:1-42
Paragraph divisions: at verses 1, 3, 10, 12, 22, 26, 32

---

1. The Feast of Passover and the Feast of Unleavened Bread constituted a double festival. Passover was celebrated on the fourteenth day of Nisan (our April); Unleavened Bread began the next and lasted for seven days. The twenty-first day of Nisan was thus the close of Passover. (The reference in 14:12 is an example of how the names of the two feasts were used interchangeably.)

A. General Analysis

1. Read the whole segment first, underlining key words and phrases in your Bible. Record these on the analytical Chart T.

2. Record the main subject of each paragraph on Chart T.

3. What is the tone, or atmosphere, of this passage?

4. Observe on Chart T that paragraph 1:3-9 is viewed here as a parenthesis in Mark's account. According to the parallel passage in John's gospel (John 12:1ff.), this anointing had taken place the Friday before ("six days before the passover").[2] Why would Mark include this story at this point?[3]

5. Analyze carefully the references to Jesus' death in each paragraph. Complete the main topical study on Chart T, under the heading "This Is My Body."

6. What does this passage teach about Jesus' opponents? About His disciples?

_____

_____

B. Paragraph Analysis

1. *Rulers' treachery (14:1-2).* What is revealed here about the religious rulers' hearts and the people's attitude toward Jesus at this time?

_____

_____

2. *Woman's devotion (14:3-9).* In what two different ways did Jesus foretell His coming death (14:7-8)?

_____

Does verse 8 suggest that the woman was consciously anticipating Jesus' death and burial by this anointing?

_____

_____

2. This follows the chronology of Albert Cassel Wieand, *A New Harmony of the Gospels* (Grand Rapids: Eerdmans, 1947).
3. Matthew 26:6-13 follows the arrangement of Mark.

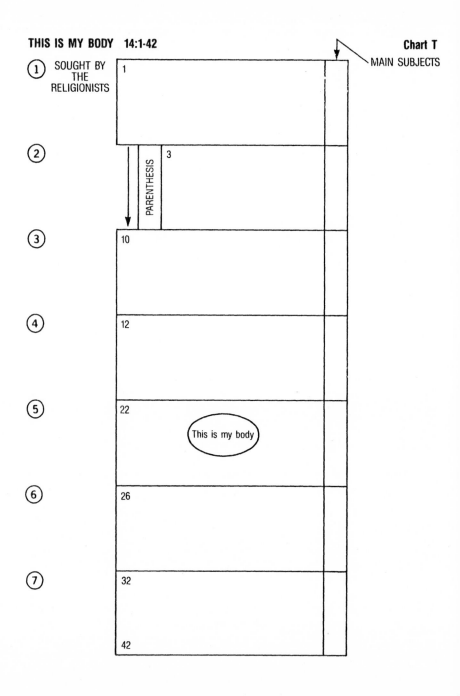

What is prophetic about the first part of verse 9?

_____

_____

3. *Judas' offer (14:10-11)*. What do you think caused Judas to want to betray Jesus? (Cf. Luke 22:3; Matt. 26:14-15.)

_____

_____

What was the reaction of the chief priests to Judas' offer?

_____

_____

What do you think were Judas' feelings at this time?

_____

_____

4. *Betrayer revealed (14:12-21)*. Compare the disciples' feelings (v. 19) with what must have been Judas's thoughts when he heard Jesus talk about a betrayer. (Cf. Matt. 26:25; John 13:23-30.)

_____

_____

5. *Last Supper (14:22-25)*. Are different meanings intended by the two statements "This is my body" (v. 22) and "This is my blood" (v. 24)?

_____

_____

What is the significance of Jesus giving thanks at this time (14:23)?

_____

_____

6. *Peter's vow (14:26-31)*. What is the key statement of the passage?

_____

_____

Read Zechariah 13:7 for the messianic prophecy of verse 27. What is the strength of the word "But" in verse 28?

_____

_____

Of this Morgan writes:

> Here immediately our Lord did that which He never failed to do; He linked the mystery of His passion with the mystery of the power which should immediately result therefrom. . . . [4]

What do verses 29-31 teach about human nature?

_____

_____

7. *Prayer in Gethsemane (14:32-42).* Make a list of the many important truths taught in this stirring paragraph.

_____

_____

What do the words "Take away this cup from me" (v. 36) reveal about Jesus?

_____

_____

Did Jesus speak the words "The hour is come" in triumph or in despair? Compare this with "Rise up, let us go."

_____

_____

III. NOTES

1. *"After two days" (14:1).* The *Berkeley* version translates verse 1 thus: "The Passover and the Feast of Unleavened Bread were due two days later."

2. *"Spikenard" (14:3).* This was a rose-red ointment made from the dried roots and stems of the nard plant, imported from northern India.

3. *"Three hundred pence" (14:5).* A pence (Roman *denarii*) was the equivalent of about eighteen cents. In those times this was a full day's wage.

4. G. Campbell Morgan, *The Gospel According to Mark*, p. 297.

4. *"An hymn" (14:26)*. Read Psalms 113-18. One of these psalms may have been the hymn sung at this time.

5. *"Take away this cup" (14:36)*. This prayer reflects the spiritual agony of the sinless One about to bear the sins of the whole world and to be smitten by the stroke of Jehovah Himself. If there had been no agony, we would wonder, "Did He *really* bear our sins in His body on the cross?"

IV. FOR THOUGHT AND DISCUSSION

1. What things can a Christian do for Christ today about which He might say, "He hath wrought a good work on me"?

2. "Why is the Lord's Supper observed by the church periodically? (See 1 Cor. 11:23-29.) Evaluate these comments: "The supreme value of the Supper of the Lord is emotional, not intellectual. . . . Our Lord said, 'This do in remembrance of Me.' The activity of memory produces the renewal of feeling, the reawakening of thanksgiving."[5] Can you think of other purposes in observing the Lord's Supper?

3. What important spiritual lessons for Christians are taught by these verses:

"He cometh, and findeth them sleeping" (14:37).

"Watch ye and pray, lest ye enter into temptation" (14:38).

V. FURTHER STUDY

Recommended subjects for study are: (1) Jesus' choice of Judas as a disciple and (2) the humanity of Jesus revealed in the Gethsemane experience.

VI. WORDS TO PONDER

The spirit truly is ready, but the flesh is weak (14:38).

Lesson 13

Arrest, Trials, and Crucifixion

Friday was D-Day for Jesus' enemies, the day scheduled for His arrest, trial, and death. Friday was very different from the five days preceding it. The first three days were active ones, when Jesus declared His authority to the multitudes; the next two days were quiet ones for Him as He ministered to His disciples, unfolding a heart of compassion. This last day, Friday, was a boisterous day of violence by the hosts of darkness when they took Christ the Lamb, the quiet, submissive one, the lonely, forsaken one, and slew Him.

There was no sleep for Jesus Thursday night. The hours until midnight were spent in prayer in the Garden of Gethsemane.[1] Then in that dark hour, and unobserved by the multitudes who were sleeping in their homes and inns, the enemies came and took Jesus by force. This arrest in Gethsename and the events that followed are the subjects of this lesson.

I. PREPARATION FOR STUDY

1. Keep in mind as you begin your study of this passage who the real opponents of Jesus are at this time. Our study thus far has revealed these to be the Jewish religious leaders. (Recall as many *group names* of these as you can.) The Roman civil rulers (e.g., Pilate) were actually drawn into the case against Jesus. Rome ruled Palestine, but a measure of home rule was allowed the local Jewish governments in the land, subject to the approval of the Roman authorities. The crime of which Jesus was accused by the Jews— blasphemy—was of a religious nature, and so the case was tried before Jewish authorities—the high priest and Sanhedrin ("council," KJV) (14:53-65; 15:1*a*). The court gave the death sentence; but

---

1. The name Gethsemane means literally "oil press."

since only the Roman civil powers could carry out such a sentence (cf. John 18:31-32), Jesus was referred to Judea's governor, Pilate (15:1*b*-19), and to King Herod, who had jurisdiction over Galilee, of which Jesus was a native.

2. Consult a Bible dictionary or encyclopedia for descriptions of the Roman punishments of scourging and crucifixion. (It is noteworthy that neither of these punishments is described in detail in the Bible. Of this Morgan comments, "I am growing impressed that the only way to come to these stories of Christ is with the self-same reticent reverence which characterized the men who wrote the story. . . . When these writers came to the [actual crucifixion], they ever dismissed it, as it seems to me, in an almost half-whisper: 'They crucified Him.'"[2])

3. Read Psalm 22, a messianic psalm prophesying Christ's crucifixion. Much of Jesus' soul and spirit experience on the cross is described here.

II. ANALYSIS

Segment to be analyzed: 14:43–15:19 and 15:20-47
Paragraph divisions: at verses 14:43, 53, 66; 15:1, 16, 20, 24, 33, 42

A. General Analysis: Arrest and Trials (14:43–15:19)

1. Read in the five paragraphs of this segment how each of the persons or groups involved in the story were alienated from Jesus:
14:43-53: Judas

Disciples

14:53-65: Members of Sanhedrin ("council")

High priest

14:66-72: Peter

15:1-15: Pilate

2. G. Campbell Morgan, *The Gospel According to Mark*, pp. 316-17.

15:16-19: Soldiers

B. Paragraph Analysis: Segment 14:43–15:19

1. *Judas' betrayal (14:43-52)*. Account for the following:
    1. The signal of Judas's kiss (v. 44).
    2. The word "safely" in Judas's directions (v. 44).
    3. The inclusion of verses 51-52. (The traditional view is that the "young man" was Mark himself.) Consider the contrasting statements "all forsook him" (v. 50) and "there followed him" (v. 51).
What does 14:48-49 teach about divine sovereignty, the Scriptures, and Christ?

_____

_____

2. *The high priest's verdict (14:53-65)*. Why do you think Jesus refused to answer the false witnesses?

_____

Note that He answered the important question of verse 61. Relate this question and Jesus' answer to the key outline of Mark (centered on 'Who Am I?").

_____

_____

What was the high priest's charge and the Sanhedrin's verdict? (14:64)

_____

_____

3. *Peter's denials (14:66-72).* Put yourself in the place of Peter. Try to think of all the things going through his mind during the period of 14:54 to 14:72.

_____

_____

What do the last two words of the paragraph reveal to you?

_____

4. *Pilate and the multitude (15:1-15).* Note that Jesus answered Pilate's question about identity (v. 2) but did not answer the false accusations (vv. 3-5). It is interesting to observe that Jesus owned the title "Christ, the Son of the Blessed" (14:61) before the highest religious body in Palestine, and the title "King of the Jews" (15:2) before the highest civil authority. What do you learn about Pilate from this account?

_____

Observe that as of this paragraph the multitudes rise up against Jesus, whereas they were still following Him a few days earlier (e.g., 12:37). What verse in this paragraph is a clue to the change?

_____

Observe the brief reference to the awful punishment of scourging, in verse 15.
5. *The soldiers contempt (15:16-19).* How was each act by the soldiers a mockery of Jesus' true royalty?

_____

_____

C. General Analysis: Crucifixion, Death, and Burial (15:20–47).

1. Chart U is a work sheet for recording your studies of this climactic passage of Mark. Observe on the chart the three main parts of the passage. Note especially the space Mark devotes to the reactions of people during the crucifixion.

1 THE JOURNEY

20

—led Him out

—Golgotha

23

2 THE CROSS

| 24 third hour: | | 33 sixth hour: ninth hour: |

| 29 —they that passed by: —chief priests: —they that were crucified with Him: 32 | MOCKERY ← REACTIONS → AWE AND DEVOTION | 39 —the centurion: —women: 41 |

3 THE TOMB

42

—craved (asked for) the body

—beheld where He was laid

47

2. Study carefully the context, meaning, and implications of the following:

"They . . . led him out to crucify him" (15:20).

"He saved others; himself he cannot save" (15:31).

Relate this verse to the key verse of Mark (10:45).

"Let Christ . . . descend now from the cross, that we may see and believe" (15:32).

"There was darkness over the whole land until the ninth hour" (15:33).

"My God, my God, why hast thou forsaken me?" (15:34).

"And the veil of the temple was rent in twain from the top to the bottom" (15:38).

"Truly this man was the Son of God" (15:39).

3. Make a comparative study of the following phrases found in the last eight verses of chapter 15:

"looking on afar off" (v. 40)

"who also, when he was in Galilee, followed him" (v. 41)

"waited for the kingdom of God" (v. 43)

"craved [requested] the body of Jesus" (v. 43)

"beheld where he was laid" (v. 47)

What picture is here portrayed of the grief and utter disappointment of some of Jesus' intimate friends?

_____

_____

_____

III. NOTES

1. *"High priest"* (14:53). The high priest was Annas, high priest emeritus who had served in the office from A.D. 6 to 15. The high priest of 14:60 was Caiaphas, son-in-law of Annas. (See John 18:13, 24.)

2. *"Council"* (14:55). The Greek word is *synedrion*, from which is derived the word "Sanhedrin." This was the high court of the Jews, composed of chief priests, scribes, and elders (cf. 15:1).

3. *"Guilty of death"* (14:64). The death penalty for blasphemy is prescribed in Leviticus 24:16.

4. *"Thou sayest it"* (15:2). Jesus was Himself answering "yes" by these words, as shown by John 18:34-38. (Read these verses.)

5. *"The third hour . . . they crucified him"* (15:25). This was 9:00 A.M. according to Jewish reckoning (whereby the day began at dawn), or 6:00 A.M. John's gospel uses Roman time (the day begin-

ning at midnight), for according to John 19:14, Pilate sentenced Jesus to be crucified in the sixth hour, or at 6:00 A.M.

6. *"Darkness over the whole land" (15:33).* Various secular writings of the first centuries report this event of darkness, such as the following description from the works of Phlegon, quoted by Eusebius: "There occurred the greatest darkening of the sun which had ever been known; it became night at mid-day, so that the stars shone in the heavens. [There was] a great earthquake in Bithynia, which destroyed a part of Nicaea."

7. *"He calleth Elias" (15:35).* The people were here referring to Jesus' cry "Eloi, Eloi" (15:34), spoken in Aramaic. The Aramaic words meant "my God, my God," but the multitudes may have intentionally confused them with the name Elias, which sounded like Eloi.

IV. FOR THOUGHT AND DISCUSSION

1. How did Jesus react to mockery, insult, and false accusation? What can Christians learn from this?

2. Ponder all that is suggested by the sentence "And when he thought thereon, he wept" (14:72). The emotional upheaval in Peter's heart was the most intense at this point. But there is a healthy work in tears, suggested by these lines of Charles Mackay:

> O ye tears, O ye tears! I am thankful that ye run;
> Though ye trickle in the darkness, ye shall glitter in the sun;
> The rainbow cannot shine if the rain refuse to fall,
> And the eyes that cannot weep are the saddest eyes of all.

3. What influence can religious leaders have on the minds and hearts of people, whether for good or evil? (cf. 15:11).

4. On the basis of your earlier study of Psalm 22, what do you think were some of the emotions of Jesus on the cross? Consider His agony of mind and heart, suggested in the words of James Salker:

> He whose very life was love, who thirsted for love as the heart pants for the water-brooks, was encircled with a sea of hatred and of dark, bitter, hellish passion, that surged round Him and flung up its waves about His cross. His soul was spotlessly pure . . . but sin pressed itself against it, endeavoring to force upon it its loathsome contact, from which it shrank through every fiber.[3]

3. James Stalkner, *The Life of Jesus Christ*, rev. ed. (Westwood, N.J.: Revell, 1891), p. 144.

115

5. In what sense was Jesus forsaken of His Father (15:34)? Consider Psalm 22:1-21 and 2 Corinthians 5:21 in answering this.

6. What is the symbolical significance of 15:38? (The veil was the thick, heavy curtain between the holy place and the most holy place, the latter entered into by the high priest only once a year.) (See Heb. 9:7-8; 10:19-22.)

V. FURTHER STUDY

1. With the aid of a harmony of the gospels, compare the four gospels' records of Friday of Passion Week. (For help in this, see *Life of Christ* [Chicago: Moody, 1969], p. 87, of this self-study series.)

2. Make a study of the various *illegal* aspects of Christ's trial. Commentaries and other books need to be consulted for this.

VI. WORDS TO PONDER

They "beheld where he was laid" (15:47).

> In that grave wherein lay the body of the dead Jesus, life was challenged, insulted, and spit upon, as it never had been before, and as it never has been since. Whatever we may feel about the tragedy of death, here it is in its most ghastly form: for here, central to human history, is a death by the side of which none other seems to be able to compare.[4]

Praise God, the Christian message does not end with Mark 15:47!

4. Morgan, p. 328.

Lesson 14

Resurrection and Final Appearances

The two closing chapters of Mark represent two climaxes in the earthly ministry of Christ. These were a climax of hate by the opposition (chap. 15) and one of vindication by God the Father (chap. 16). Jesus never faltered in pressing the claim that He was the Christ, the Son of the living God. When Peter so recognized Him in answer to the question, "But you, who do *you* say I am?" (8:29, *Berkeley*), Jesus turned His face to Jerusalem with one thing in mind: to die and to rise from the dead (8:31).

The crucifixion of Jesus was a triumph for Him only because His resurrection on the third day was a reality. Mark 15 records the historical fact of Jesus' vicariously dying for the sins of the whole world, presenting Himself to God His Father as an atoning sacrifice. Mark 16 records the historical fact of God's accepting that sacrifice by raising His Son from the dead. Either event would have been meaningless without the other, so it does not surprise us to see how careful Jesus was when foretelling His approaching death (8:31ff.), to foretell His resurrection in the same breath, as it were.

Lesson 12 ended with the sad and desolate picture of two women beholding the tomb where the body of Jesus was laid. This last lesson of our study is the bright and glorious sequel.

I. PREPARATION FOR STUDY

1. You might want to review all the chapters of Mark leading up to this last one for a renewed appreciation of Jesus' ministry for mankind and for a deeper conviction that His resurrection was inevitable. Review the survey Chart D, including the comparison of the phrases "Jesus came" (chap. 1) and "He was received up" (chap. 16).

2. As you begin your study of chapter 16, try to enter into the feelings of Jesus' close friends, relatives, and disciples who had mourned His death and were not expecting to see Him again.

II. ANALYSIS

Segment to be analyzed: 16:1-20[1]
Paragraph divisions: at verses 1, 9, 14, 19

A. General Analysis

1. After you have marked off the paragraph divisions in your Bible, read the whole chapter for overall impressions.
2. Compare these two experiences of the women:
  "beheld where he was laid" (15:47)
  "saw that the stone was rolled away" (16:4)
3. Chart V is a partly completed analytical chart to be used for recording further observations as you continue your analysis. Read 16:1-8 again. Do you think that Mark would have a natural conclusion if the book ended at verse 8?[2]

_____

_____

Note the repeated word "appeared" in the Bible text of 16:9-18. Does this relate in any way to the promise of verse 7?

_____

What is the geographical reference in verse 7?

_____

_____

The appearances of Jesus reported in verse 9-13 were in or around Jerusalem. It is possible that all or part of the words of

---

1. The section 16:9-20 is not accepted by all textual scholars as having been written by Mark, because it is lacking in some of the best ancient Greek manuscripts. Much has been written on the pros and cons of this question. This writer accepts the passage as a divinely purposed conclusion to the gospel, whoever the human author may have been.
2. Some old manuscripts add a short ending beyond verse 8. (See TEV for an example of one.)

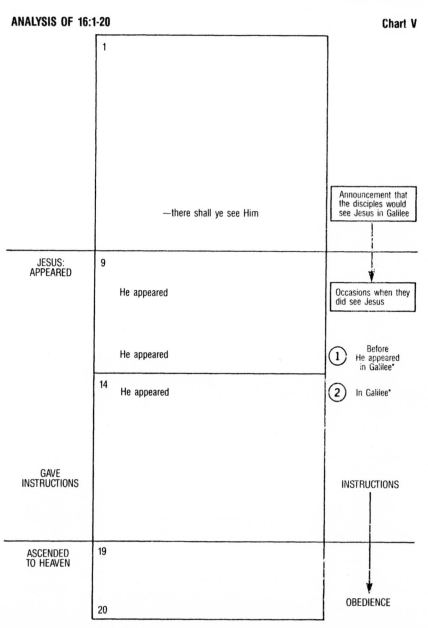

*See the Analysis section for this identification of Galilee.

16:14-18 were spoken by Jesus in Galilee.[3] If this is so, the latter verses are a fulfillment of the promise of verse 7 (so indicated on Chart V).[4]

4. Observe the three things reported here about Jesus: His appearances, His instructions to the eleven disciples, and His ascension.

B. Paragraph Analysis

1. *Paragraph 16:1-8.* What different aspects of Jesus' life work are suggested by these words of verse 6:

Jesus of Nazareth:

_____

crucified:

_____

risen:

_____

not here:

_____

Do you think the stone had been rolled back (16:4) to let Jesus out of the sepulcher?

_____

_____

What were the instructions of verse 7?

_____

_____

Why did the women not carry them out?

_____

_____

2. *Paragraph 16:9-13.* What evidences of belief and unbelief do you see here?

_____

_____

3. See Henry Alford, *The Greek Testament*, 1:435-36; also A.T. Robertson, *A Harmony of the Gospels for Students of the Life of Christ* (Nashville: Broadman, 1922), p. 249.
4. Passages clearly identifying Jesus' Galilean appearances are John 21 and Matt. 28:16-20. Robertson places the appearances of 1 Cor. 15:6 in Galilee also (ibid.)

3. *Paragraph 16:14-18.* For what did Jesus reprove His disciples?

_____

Analyze carefully the commission which He gave His disciples (vv. 15-18).

_____

From your acquaintance with the book of Acts, did any of the signs of verses 17-18 attend the ministry of the gospel in those early decades (e.g., see Acts 28:1-6)?

_____

What is the main function of such signs (cf. 16:20; Heb. 2:4.)

_____

What was the main function of Jesus' miracles during His public ministry?

_____

4. *The concluding paragraph of Mark (16:19-20).* What important and wonderful truths are taught in these verses?

"So then	
—after the Lord . . . —He was received up into heaven, —and sat on the right hand of God.	had spoken unto them, And they went forth, and preached everywhere,
the Lord working with them, and confirming the word with signs following. Amen."	

_____

_____

_____

III. NOTES

1. *"A young man" (16:5).* This is the angel of Matthew 28:5. In all, there were two angels (Luke 24:4).

2. *"And Peter"* (16:7). Jesus singled out Peter intentionally. What was probably His reason?

_____

_____

3. *"He goeth before you into Galilee"* (16:7). The appearances in Galilee took place toward the end of the forty-day postresurrection period.

IV. FOR THOUGHT AND DISCUSSION

1. Does Mark teach the literal, bodily resurrection of Jesus? Can there be an "Easter faith" without the "Easter fact"?

2. Must the miracle of Christ's resurrection be fully understood to be accepted? Does the Bible explain the process of the resurrection? Evaluate these comments of Morgan on the Easter story as preached in the twentieth century:

> The resurrection is a fact that cannot be proved, except to the faith of the heart. The resurrection cannot be proved mechanically, mathematically, by the demonstration of our small clevernesses. . . . No man knows Jesus rose from the dead, save the man who in helplessness of soul has trusted Him, and has received that spiritual mystic, inner witness, that knows no denial, and laughs at criticism.[5]

3. What does the resurrection mean to you, in a practical way? What did it mean to the apostles of the book of Acts?

4. What is the gospel's message of salvation (16:15-16)? Is the rite of water baptism a requirement for salvation? (Cf. Rom. 3:28; Eph. 2:8-9.)

V. FURTHER STUDY

Study 1 Corinthians 15, which is the Bible's classic interpretation of the doctrine of Christ's resurrection and the believer's resurrection.

A Concluding Word

The empty tomb of Mark 16 is a witness to the world that there *truly is* a "gospel of Jesus Christ, the Son of God" (1:1). The dilemma of every human being since the Fall of Adam has been and is

5. G. Campbell Morgan, *The Gospel According to Mark*, p. 342.

still this: "I want to live, but I must die." There is absolutely only one solution for this dilemma, and that is found in THE GOSPEL OF JESUS CHRIST. It was this Jesus who "bent over the corpse of the dead world, and whispered a word of faith . . . words until then unknown: Love, Sacrifice, a heavenly origin."[6]

It is my hope that you are among those who have this new life in Christ. May your study of the gospel of Mark have brought you even a measure of the warmth and joy that John Mark must have experienced as he was inspired to write it.

6. G. Mazzini, p. 15.

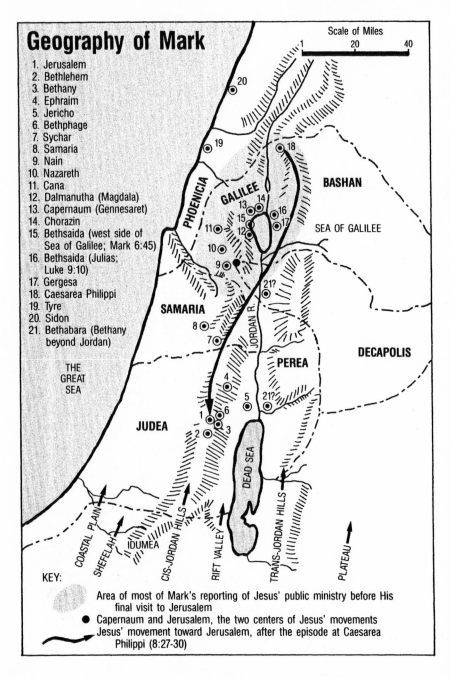

Geography of Mark

1. Jerusalem
2. Bethlehem
3. Bethany
4. Ephraim
5. Jericho
6. Bethphage
7. Sychar
8. Samaria
9. Nain
10. Nazareth
11. Cana
12. Dalmanutha (Magdala)
13. Capernaum (Gennesaret)
14. Chorazin
15. Bethsaida (west side of Sea of Galilee; Mark 6:45)
16. Bethsaida (Julias; Luke 9:10)
17. Gergesa
18. Caesarea Philippi
19. Tyre
20. Sidon
21. Bethabara (Bethany beyond Jordan)

Scale of Miles

THE GREAT SEA

PHOENICIA

GALILEE

BASHAN

SEA OF GALILEE

SAMARIA

JORDAN R.

PEREA

DECAPOLIS

JUDEA

DEAD SEA

COASTAL PLAIN

SHEFELAH

IDUMEA

CIS-JORDAN HILLS

RIFT VALLEY

TRANS-JORDAN HILLS

PLATEAU

KEY:

Area of most of Mark's reporting of Jesus' public ministry before His final visit to Jerusalem

● Capernaum and Jerusalem, the two centers of Jesus' movements

Jesus' movement toward Jerusalem, after the episode at Caesarea Philippi (8:27-30)

124

Bibliography

SELECTED SOURCES FOR FURTHER STUDY

Blaiklock, E. M. *Mark: The Man and His Message*. Chicago: Moody, 1967.

Davidson, F.; Stibbs, A. M.; and Kevan, E. F. *The New Bible Commentary*. Grand Rapids: Eerdmans, 1953.

Earle, Ralph. *Mark: The Gospel of Action*. Everyman's Bible Commentary. Chicago: Moody, 1970.

Jensen, Irving L. *Life of Christ*. Chicago: Moody, 1969.

Lange, John Peter. "Mark." In the *Commentary on the Holy Scriptures*. Vol. 2. Reprint. Grand Rapids: Zondervan, n.d.

Lenski, R. C. H. *The Interpretation of Mark*. Columbus, O.: Wartburg, 1946.

Morgan, G. Campbell. *The Gospel According to Mark*. Westwood, N.J.: Revell, 1927. Unexcelled for its thematic studies in the gospel.

————— *The Parables and Metaphors of Our Lord*. Westwood, N.J.: Revelle, 1943.

Moule, C. F. D. *The Gospel According to Mark*. The Cambridge Bible Commentary. Cambridge: U. Press, 1965.

Pfeiffer, Charles F., and Harrison, Everett F., eds. *The Wycliffe Bible Commentary*. Chicago: Moody, 1962.

Robertson, A. T. *Word Pictures in the New Testament*. Vol. 1. New York: Harper, 1930.

Swete, Henry Barclay. *The Gospel According to St. Mark*. Grand Rapids: Eerdmans, 1951. A technical commentary on the Greek text.

Taylor, Vincent. *The Gospel According to St. Mark*. London: Macmillan, 1953.

Tenney, Merrill C. *The Zondervan Pictorial Bible Dictionary*. Grand Rapids: Zondervan, 1963.

Unger, Merrill F. *Unger's Bible Dictionary*. Chicago: Moody, 1957.
_____. *Unger's Bible Handbook*. Chicago: Moody, 1966.
Vincent, Marvin R. *Word Studies in the New Testament*. Vol. 1. Grand Rapids: Eerdmans, 1946.
Vine, W. E. *An Expository Dictionary of New Testament Words*. Westwood, N.J.: Revell, 1961.
Wuest, Kenneth S. *Mark in the Greek New Testament*. Grand Rapids: Eerdmans, 1950.

Printed in the United States
1393000001B/189